# STAR WARS

# STAR WARS

## THE TRIUMPH OF NERD CULTURE

*Josef Benson*

ROWMAN & LITTLEFIELD
*Lanham • Boulder • New York • London*

Published by Rowman & Littlefield
An imprint of The Rowman & Littlefield Publishing Group, Inc.
4501 Forbes Boulevard, Suite 200, Lanham, Maryland 20706
www.rowman.com

6 Tinworth Street, London, SE11 5AL, United Kingdom

British Library Cataloguing in Publication Information Available

**Library of Congress Cataloging-in-Publication Data**

Names: Benson, Josef, 1974– author.
Title: Star Wars : the triumph of nerd culture / Josef Benson.
Description: Lanham : Rowman & Littlefield, [2020] | Includes bibliographical
    references and index. | Summary: "Star Wars: The Triumph of Nerd Culture seeks
    to tell the story of the film franchise from the point of view of the fans who had as
    much to do with making the film what it is today as the film itself."—Provided by
    publisher.
Identifiers: LCCN 2020011295 (print) | LCCN 2020011296 (ebook) | ISBN
    9781538116203 (cloth) | ISBN 9781538116210 (epub)
Subjects: LCSH: Star Wars films—History and criticism. | Star War fans—United
    States | Star Wars films—Social aspects—United States. | Star Wars films—
    Collectibles—United States.
Classification: LCC PN1995.9.S695 B46 2020  (print) | LCC PN1995.9.S695
    (ebook) | DDC 791.43/75—dc23
LC record available at https://lccn.loc.gov/2020011295
LC ebook record available at https://lccn.loc.gov/2020011296

♾™ The paper used in this publication meets the minimum requirements of
American National Standard for Information Sciences—Permanence of Paper
for Printed Library Materials, ANSI/NISO Z39.48-1992.

*For my son Laz.*
*May the force be with you, always.*

# CONTENTS

# ACKNOWLEDGMENTS

Many thanks to Stephen Ryan for his hard work on this project. Thank you to my brother Cory Benson for his invaluable contributions. Also, thanks to my boy Laz, whose love for *Star Wars* allowed me to experience it for the first time again.

# PROLOGUE

## The Triumph of Nerd Culture

After nearly two decades of planning and one year of intense construction, on July 17, 1955, Disneyland opened in Anaheim, California. Creator Walt Disney successfully transformed 160 acres of orange groves into a $17 million theme park. Walt Disney sold vacation property and borrowed against his life insurance in order to finance the project that some in Hollywood referred to as Walt's folly. In addition to the over 28,000 people that passed through the gates on that day, over 70 million more watched the park open on Disney's popular weekly show on ABC, called *Disneyland*. Ronald Reagan hosted the unveiling, and the show featured a who's who of Hollywood royalty, including Sammy Davis Jr. and Frank Sinatra. While the show went off without a hitch, unfolding like a fantasyland before the gaze of millions, the reality was quite different. Temperatures reached nearly a hundred degrees, and many of the park attractions were inoperative. All three restaurants and many of the refreshment stands ran out of food and beverages for customers. Despite the initial problems, it only took seven weeks for a million customers to enter the "Magic Kingdom."[1] A *Los Angeles Times* article appearing just two days after the grand opening titled "Disneyland Opens Gates to Thousands" noted that the park opened up at 10:00 a.m. to 15,000 waiting park-goers, some of whom had been waiting all night. The eager throngs formed a line, four abreast, that stretched a mile long outside ten turnstiles. The first two customers were a seven-year-old boy and a five-year-old girl. Walt Disney himself was on hand to greet the children. Disney gave away lifetime passes to the two kids at the head of the line and their families as a way to reward their enthusiasm. Once the park opened, there was standing room only as far as the eye could see. As the big day wore on, complications arose, such as the dishwashing machine in one restaurant break-ing down and a gas main leak in Fantasyland.[2]

Less than one month after opening day, Vice President Richard Nixon vis-ited the wondrous theme park. Nixon arrived with his wife and two daughters. As the vice president took off on a pirate ship to Never Land, his wife noted, "Dick's getting a bigger kick out of this than the kids."[3]

The story of Disneyland is not unlike the story of *Star Wars*, insofar as one man's unwavering vision and ambition resulted in great success despite hic-cups along the way. Perhaps this comparison is no coincidence, since among the kids at Disneyland on opening day was an eleven-year-old George Lucas. His family not only came the first day, but they stayed an entire week. Lucas noted, "I loved Disneyland . . . I wandered around. I'd go on the rides and the bumper cars, the steam boats, the shooting galleries, the jungle rides . . . I was in heaven."[4]

Thirty years later, in February 1985, Disney and Lucasfilm formally an-nounced an agreement whereby they would work together on attractions for the theme park, including a *Star Wars* ride called "Star Tours." The ride employed military-grade flight simulators to give customers the feeling that they were flying through the *Star Wars* universe for four and a half minutes, engaging in dogfights with TIE Fighters and attacking the Death Star. The ride opened in 1987, and Lucas returned to the same Disneyland that he had visited on opening day to cut the ribbon. Once the ride opened, it ran at capacity for sixty hours straight. Lucas offered, "I've always felt that there's only one first-class amusement park operation, and this is it. . . . When I did something, I've always wanted to make sure it was done right. . . . This is the only place in the world like that."[5]

Twenty-four years later, in May 2011, Lucas traveled to Walt Disney World in Orlando, Florida, to attend the reopening of "Star Tours," the at-traction that he helped create for the park in 1987. That morning, Lucas met with Bob Iger, chief executive officer of the Walt Disney Company and the man who had already brought Pixar and Marvel to Disney. The two met in 1991 when Iger was working for ABC and greenlit Lucas's show, *The Young Indiana Jones Chronicles*.

At the Hollywood Brown Derby restaurant in Orlando, over an omelet George had ordered and a yogurt parfait for Iger, Iger popped a ludicrous ques-tion to Lucas: Would George be willing to sell Lucasfilm to Disney?[6] After a few moments, George said no, that he was not there yet but would love to talk again if he changed his mind.

The following January, Lucas told *New York Times* reporter Bryan Curtis, "I'm moving away from the business, from the company, from all this kind of stuff." Once again Lucas weakly mentioned that he was still interested in making his personal, experimental films, something that he had been saying since the 1970s. When asked whether there would be any more *Star Wars* movies, Lucas revealed the real reason for stepping away: "Why would I make any more when everybody yells at you all the time and says what a terrible person you are. . . . With the internet, it's gotten very vicious and personal. . . . You just say to yourself, why do I need to do this?"[7] Lucas also added that there would never be episodes VII through IX, erroneously suggesting that *Star Wars* began and ended with him. This was far from the truth, and one reason why he was completely disillusioned in the first place. He had created something that would go on with or without him. The vituperative fan criticism that he received regarding the prequels clearly jaded him and was in no small part his own fault for a number of alleged betrayals of *Star Wars* fandom.

Lucas noticed that when Steve Jobs sold Pixar to Disney, Disney treated Jobs's company reverently and ran it exactly as Jobs had. In addition to buying Pixar in 2006, Disney CEO Bob Iger also bought Marvel. Lucas was intimately familiar with these two companies, having created the first and helped keep afloat the second. Iger allowed these awesome companies to retain their idiosyncratic cultures. Iger clearly had Lucas's attention.

Lucas was not ready to sell, largely because he did not have the leadership in place to replace him. He needed to identify a successor to run the company when he let it go. Kathleen Kennedy was one of the most successful producers in Hollywood, and Steven Spielberg's longtime production partner. In the spring of 2012, Lucas took Kennedy to lunch and told her that he was aggressively moving toward retirement. He asked her if she would be interested in taking over the company. Kennedy already ran a successful production company called Amblin Entertainment that she cofounded with Spielberg. She told Lucas the answer was yes.

Lucas realized that the best way to drum up the value of his franchise was to create more *Star Wars* films. Despite declaring on numerous occasions that there would be no further episodes beyond the first six, Lucas began writing again. He contacted Mark Hamill, Carrie Fisher, and Harrison Ford and began negotiations. He also called on Lawrence Kasdan, who wrote *The Empire Strikes Back* and *Return of the Jedi*. Lucasfilm announced Kennedy's promotion to cochair of Lucasfilm on June 1, 2012. With the wheels in motion for more *Star Wars* films and new leadership in place, Lucas was finally ready to sell.

Over twenty Disney lawyers sprang into action in order to ascertain that Lucas actually owned the entire franchise. They created files on all the characters and interrogated agreements dating back to the early 1970s. Iger insisted on no leaks as the deal began to take shape. The final hitch centered on Lucas's refusal to let Iger see any of the new treatments for future *Star Wars* films. Iger wanted to make sure that Lucas actually had written treatments for future films. Lucas decided to play hardball, just as he had when he was a kid and negotiated with the neighborhood kids the price of admission to the haunted house in his garage. He told *BusinessWeek*, "Buying my stories is part of what the deal is. I've worked at this for 40 years, and I've been pretty successful. I mean, I could have said, fine, well, I'll just sell the company to somebody else."[8] Lucas only partially relented, allowing just three people to see the treatments—Iger, Disney Chair Alan Horn, and Vice President Kevin Mayer. In a gesture that was an omen of things to come, Iger's response to the treatments was tepid at best, allowing only that they had lots of potential. Iger's final act before making a decision was to watch all six films in a row over one weekend in October, after which he made his decision.

On October 19, 2012, Lucas turned the camera on himself in order to obviate the need for any interviews regarding the sale. In front of him was Kathleen Kennedy. The idea was to officially pass the torch to Kennedy and release the footage on YouTube. Lucas wiggled out of his earlier declaration that there would be no more *Star Wars* films by sheepishly saying, "I always said I wasn't going to do any more, and that's true, because I'm not going to do them. . . . That doesn't mean I'm unwilling to turn it over to Kathleen to do more."[9]

George's initial offer was to hand over the entire company to Iger and Disney while maintaining complete control. George wanted to have his cake and eat it, too. Iger refused, telling Lucas that if he sold the franchise, Disney would have final say. Lucas acquiesced and agreed to sell under the condition that Disney agreed to consult his story treatments for future films, an indication of the filmmaker's reluctance to let go. On October 30, 2012, Lucas and Iger signed the agreement that transferred ownership of Lucasfilm from Lucas to Disney for $4.05 billion, half in cash and half in Disney stock, making Lucas one of Disney's largest stakeholders with 2 percent ownership of the company. In January 2013, Lucasfilm announced that J. J. Abrams would direct *Star Wars: Episode VII*. The news buoyed Disney stock to a record high. Lucas achieved what he set out to do, making *Star Wars* as valuable as he could before reaping the benefits from his newly acquired stock shares.

The reporting around the time of the sale largely focused on Disney's transition from a company that created its intellectual content in-house to one that paid billions of dollars for existing characters. An article in the *Los Angeles Times*, "Disney Adds *Star Wars* to Its Galaxy: The Big-Bucks Deal for Lucasfilm Will Enable It to Exploit the Film Series through Sequels, TV, and Theme Parks," made no effort to hide its disdain for Disney's exploitation of built-in markets like *Star Wars*. Disney's new business strategy was to capitalize on the *Star Wars* franchise's exceptional risk-proof fandom. In the article, Ben Fritz and Richard Verrier not so subtly lamented the new direction of the juggernaut company from one that mostly created in-house art to one that gobbled up popular characters from other franchises.[10] In another *Los Angeles Times* article dated November 11, 2012, Neal Gabler took the idea one step further, suggesting that Disney's purchase of Lucasfilm marked a transition in the filmmaking industry overall as studios transitioned from the entertainment industry to the branding industry.[11] Lucasfilm had developed into one of the premier *brands* in the world, rather than a franchise that produced great movies.

When studios reigned supreme, not long before Lucas made his way into the industry, the films themselves were the primary artifact that the studios sold. Audiences went to the movies to see particular stars and, to a lesser degree, writers and directors. Nearly every film was a measured risk. Walt Disney changed the industry when he began merchandising his brand beyond the films themselves in an attempt to alleviate some of the risk involved in filmmaking. As films became more financially risky, studios such as Disney became more interested in the business side of things. When Disney purchased Marvel Comics and *Star Wars*, they were interested in replicating the branding that had been successful for them in the past. Marvel Comics and *Star Wars* had proven to be enduring brands that audiences loved. Rather than films creating brands, now brands created the films. The ominous aspect of this commercial equation was that there was no real need for the films themselves to be any good in the short term. If the brand was strong, which it certainly was in the case of Marvel and *Star Wars*, then the fans would come no matter what. The only risk was that eventually the brand would falter as the product weakened. In Disney, Lucas saw a paragon franchise that parlayed stories and characters into big business. Disney was known for its parks and toys as much as its films. Likewise, the reach of *Star Wars* went way beyond the films themselves. Disney and *Star Wars* were kindred corporations.

It is perhaps facile to suggest that Lucas sold Lucasfilm to Disney simply because he thought Disney was a first-rate kindred company that he trusted, or because he wanted the kind of generational money that he received. All that is likely true, but that does not explain why a man who already had all the money that he could ever spend in a lifetime would sell the one thing that defined him not only as an artist but also as a man. Lucas once noted that his only regret was that he was the only nerd in the world who could not stand in line and wait for the new *Star Wars* movie.[12] Lucas never wanted to simply drift back into the folds of nerd culture and stand in line waiting for the next *Star Wars* movie. The fans themselves drove Lucas to sell. *Star Wars* fandom has always played a major role in the story of *Star Wars*. Just as there is a riveting saga within the *Star Wars* universe that centers on the rise and fall of Anakin Skywalker and the redemption of Darth Vader, so has a saga unfolded regarding George Lucas and *Star Wars* fandom. The *Star Wars* saga beyond the films centers on the rise and fall of George Lucas and the triumph of nerd culture.

# 1

# AREN'T YOU A LITTLE SHORT FOR A STORMTROOPER?

George Lucas was always a nerd. Born on Sunday May 14, 1944, he was small—five pounds and fourteen ounces—but feisty.[1] His parents right away began describing the would-be famous director and multibillionaire as "scrawny." They also noted his protruding ears. One ear was even a little floppy, but George Sr. soon had it taped up and eventually proclaimed it a good ear. George Jr.'s diminutive stature and prominent ears would become his defining physical traits as he grew up—traits that, fairly or not, marked him as a nerd. Lucas's nerdiness, present from the moment of his birth, would be a driving factor in the creation of one of the biggest film franchises the world has ever known as well as a driving factor in its destruction.

George Lucas Sr. arrived in Modesto, California, in 1929, one of the final stops of the Central Pacific Railroad before it headed on to Los Angeles and Sacramento. In high school, George Sr. met and fell in love with Dorothy Bomberger, the pride and joy of one of Modesto's oldest and wealthiest families. The elder George was very conservative and felt it was his duty alone to support his growing family. The aspiring patriarch eventually found work at Modesto's primary stationery business, L. M. Morris Company. While the store sold large domestic items like furniture, it eventually began selling cameras, projectors, books, and toys. George Sr. eventually took over the store as primary owner and provided the upper-middle-class life he desired for his growing family that included his wife, two daughters, and son George Jr.

George Jr. experienced a formative and spiritual epiphany when he was only six years old. He attended Sunday school every week and eventually came to loathe it. He described his spiritual awakening as "very profound." According to Lucas, "It centered around God" and he found himself asking questions like "What is God?" and "What is reality?"[2] Psychologists often point to a significant occurrence in a child's life when they realize that their body is a fragmented part of the world, that their perspective on the world is not actually the entire world itself. The child then realizes that other people can view them individually and mark them as different or inadequate. This realization is both exciting and terrifying. Children become aware of the power of their subjectivity as well as their own vulnerability. For much of his life, Lucas has been both powerful and exceptionally sensitive, forever capitalizing on the opportunity to make sense of the world and lamenting his own fragility.

As Lucas matured, he both embraced his father's patriarchal conservatism and rebelled against it. George Lucas Sr. was the most important influence on George Lucas Jr.'s life. George Sr. felt it was a man's duty and obligation to work and support his family while his wife and the mother of his children stayed home and looked after the kids. Even though the elder Lucas was willing to give George just about anything he wanted, it always came at a price, paid by listening to lectures on frugality and hard work.

George Lucas Jr. made good on the nerd potential provided by his diminutive stature. He loved gadgets, science fiction, technology, and comic books. Because his father was a successful stationer in Modesto, George Jr. was able to get the newest toys and novelties. As a kid, Lucas and his friends used these toys to build communities and tableaus that he called environments, setting them up in wood and glass cases.[3] Everyone in the neighborhood knew that George had the best toys because his old man ran the stationery store and ordered the newest and coolest stuff. Lucas and his best friend, John Plummer, built environments that were little more than boxes in which they would create miniature scenes involving race cars and figurines. Lucas had a shed out back with tools that he used to create these scenes and stoke his already burning desire for make-believe. George also displayed an entrepreneurial spirit by creating entire carnivals in his backyard with games and rides, including a small roller coaster as well as a haunted house in his garage that he would charge a fee to enter.[4] He would change it up so neighborhood kids would want to try it a second and third time.[5] He employed the same strategy later in life with his films, park attractions, and tie-in toys. Lucas once told an interviewer, "I'm very much akin to a toy-maker. If I wasn't a filmmaker, I'd probably *be* a toy-maker."[6] It is not a stretch to think of Lucas's films *as* toys, the line between the films themselves and the tie-in toys blurry at best, a business strategy similar to that employed by the Disney Corporation.

When asked about Lucas, one classmate noted that George was a nonentity in school who simply did not make much of an impression despite being relatively popular. A measure of that popularity was likely due to his access to toys and the carnivals that he created in his backyard. George had the best train set in the neighborhood, a three-engine Lionel Santa Fe model with all the trappings.[7] Money and its power has been a recurring element in George Lucas's life. Despite Lucas's lifelong claim that his financial success was a fluke, his relationship with money was evident from the beginning, along with his affinity for making it.

Lucas also had a comic book connection in his buddy John Plummer, whose dad procured thousands of unsold comic books from one of his friends who ran a local newsstand. These comics were marked as unsold by their missing covers. George often hung out all day and into the evening on his buddy's porch well after John had gone inside for dinner, poring over comic books. This was the early 1950s "golden age" of comic books, when there was very little regulation and titles sold in the millions.

Lucas also loved the Saturday morning serials that featured short films depicting the adventures of Flash Gordon. George preferred the science fiction comics to the superhero comics, and it was the *Flash Gordon* serials he had in mind when he was thinking about creating a science fiction movie of his own.[8] The *Flash Gordon* serials released by Universal in 1936, 1938, and 1940 were episodic, and eventually aired in syndication on American television in the 1950s, where they came to the attention of a young George Lucas. Each episode began with introductory text that situated the viewer *in medias res* within the story about to unfold, similar to the familiar crawl at the beginning of Lucas's *Star Wars* films. *Flash Gordon* was quintessential space opera as Flash, the main character played by Buster Crabbe and sometimes referred to as "Earth Man," often found himself in constant conflict with Emperor Ming the Merciless, a classic villain not unlike the emperor in *Star Wars*. Other stylistic similarities between the *Flash Gordon* serials and *Star Wars* include transitional swipes and actors playing their roles straight in the midst of silly costumes and props, such as obviously fake fire-breathing dragons. Dr. Hans Zarkov forces Yale student Flash and his girlfriend Dale to travel to the planet Mongo in order to prevent its collision with Earth. While there, Flash and the others encounter the ruler of Mongo, Ming the Merciless. Flash Gordon possesses no superpowers, and his plight is plot driven in terms of preventing Earth's collision with Mongo. Notwithstanding the many similarities to the *Flash Gordon* serials, one important difference in the *Star Wars* universe is its complete removal from the known world. There is no such thing as Yale University or Earth in the *Star Wars* universe.

Other kids on the block often bullied George, compelling his sister Wendy to come to his rescue. Some neighborhood kids once held him down, removed his shoes, and threw them into a sprinkler-soaked lawn. Wendy came to his aid, scared off the other boys, and retrieved George's shoes.[9] If young George got away with only having his "shoes" removed, then he was lucky. The likelier scenario was that the other boys "pantsed" him, or yanked his underwear right off his body with his pants still on, humiliating him in front of the other kids. Like many victims of bullying, the experience was certainly traumatic for George Lucas Jr. and something he would carry with him for the rest of his life.

The bullying that Lucas endured as a young man, in addition to his later lack of sexual success, had a tremendous effect on his handling of the *Star Wars* franchise as well as *Star Wars* fandom. For him, *Star Wars* supplanted what he would normally have derived from sexual conquest. *Star Wars* became the source of his self-esteem and, when it no longer provided that, he got rid of it.

Early bullying often causes a lack of self-esteem for the victim. Positive self-esteem engenders happiness, stability, and achievement. Conversely, a lack of self-esteem due to childhood trauma can derail well-being and cause bitterness and failure. Often self-esteem is tied to sexual confidence. A man who is confident in his own masculinity flourishes, while the man who does not think highly of himself is often bitter and intolerant. Unless he can crack his negative self-image and replace it with one that he can feel proud of, he is likely to nurse resentment all his life. Even those who have a healthy self-regard often need to have it constantly reaffirmed by sexual conquest. Otherwise, the sexually inadequate man may revert to his grim dark prison of frustration and anger, glowering at the world outside that denies him the right to self-assertion.

George Sr. was exceedingly strict and every bit the conservative patriarch of the family. He made George get a crewcut every year and generally thought his son would bloom late, if at all. George Sr. felt that George was a mama's boy.[10] Young George responded to his domineering father by latching on to other big brother figures, such as his older sister Anne's boyfriend. Lucas was infatuated with the man. When Anne's boyfriend was killed in Korea, George was crushed.

Lucas described his childhood once as tough and repressed, filled with fear and trepidation.[11] The death of Anne's boyfriend had a tremendous effect on George, and he would return to the idea of young men killed in war in his first successful film, *American Graffiti*, as well as in the *Star Wars* saga.

Lucas's buddy John Plummer noted that Lucas never dated. Plummer said Lucas thought dating was dumb. However, Plummer also related that Lucas was interested in stereotypical blondes, "Debbie-type girls."[12] Lucas himself admitted that he never had a high school girlfriend. Lucas found an outlet for his desire to escape mundane Modesto through fantasy, whether that was in his environments, comic books, Disneyland, or television. These fantasies likely involved romance, heroism, and science fiction and would eventually make their way into his films.

In 1958 Lucas was fourteen years old, one hundred pounds soaking wet, and five feet six inches, the tallest he would ever be. In school photos, he was always in the front row.[13] The thing to do in Modesto was cruising. Lucas claimed to have lost his virginity in the back of a car with a girl from one of the tougher high schools, Modesto High, but no one ever claimed to have been his girlfriend.

Despite Lucas's small frame and interest in decidedly nerdy stuff like science fiction and comic books, he had a rebellious streak. In school, he was not a good student. Before he was sixteen, George already started letting his hair grow long and sported black boots with silver tips and black Levis that he wore for weeks at a time without washing. In high school, he began hanging around with the local kids who were into cars and considered lower class. After pestering his folks, they finally bought him a car, an Autobianchi equipped with just a two-cylinder engine—little more than a sewing machine, Lucas lamented. He rolled the car once before he even got his license and had to have it towed to Modesto's Foreign Car Service, where Plummer worked. For weeks, he and John souped up the little car until it was finally passable as a decent set of wheels. After that, he and John began racing all the time.

George and his father often did not see eye to eye, especially when it came to George's future. The tension between father and son came to a head when Lucas turned eighteen and refused to continue working at his father's stationery store. Young George worked at the store for a short time but soon quit, infuriating the old man. Lucas told his dad that he would never work at a job that was so boring. For George Sr., the family business was George's birthright. He had worked hard to give his son the business, and for George to refuse it was tantamount to an indictment of his father's life's work. Nevertheless, George Sr. acquiesced, but not before telling George that he would likely come crawling back for the job, to which George responded that not only would he not change his mind but that he would be a millionaire before he was thirty. He knew he never wanted to be the president of a company. His future was in cars. As it turned out, the only prediction that came true was George Jr. achieving millionaire status before he was thirty.

Meanwhile, Lucas was gaining a reputation as a poor student and a general hell raiser, accumulating traffic tickets once he got his license and making himself known to local law enforcement. He was too young at the time to race professionally in Northern California, where drivers in the autocross circuit who raced against a clock instead of other drivers had to be at least twenty-one. This dynamic would be the subject of one of Lucas's early films, *1:42:08*, which he made in his senior year at the University of Southern California. Autocross was the first step into the world of NASCAR.

Instead of racing, Lucas became the personal mechanic of Allen Grant. Four years Lucas's elder, good looking, and a lady's man, Grant gained lots of attention from big-time sponsors when driving his Ford Mustang Cobra. Lucas's interest in cars and racing sprang from his interest in mechanical toys like his train set. His interest in the cultural aspects of racing, such as the look and behavior of car guys, allowed him to break free from his own nerdy identity conferred by Lucas's classmates from Downey High, who described him as "a nerd, but . . . very nice." Another remembered Lucas reading comic books between classes. Yet another classmate recalled him hiding behind his camera at sporting events and calling him a little dork.[14]

By the end of his senior year, he was in danger of not graduating. On June 12, 1962, he decided to go to the library to study. Just before George got home, a Chevy Impala, driven by a seventeen-year-old, T-boned his little sportscar just as he was turning into the dirt road to his house, sending it rolling and eventually exploding into a walnut tree. Lucas was flung from the car because the seatbelt that he made malfunctioned. Amazingly, he only sustained a gash to his forehead and a bruised and hemorrhaged lung along with a few minor fractures. Given the state of his car, he should have been dead. Many of his classmates thought he had been killed. His mangled car was hauled onto a flatbed truck and taken away as junk. All his teachers who had planned to fail him instead passed him sympathetically. Lucas spent the next four months in the hospital and for the second time experienced a life-changing existential epiphany. The failure of the protective racing belt that he had made for the car had saved him. Lucas noted,

> I was in an accident that, in theory, no one could survive. . . . So it was like, Well, I'm here, and every day now is an extra day. I've been given an extra day so I've got to make the most of it. And then the next day I began with *two* extra days. . . . You can't help in that situation but get into the mindset like that. . . . You've been given this gift and every single day is a gift. And I wanted to make the most of it. . . . It was almost starting a new life.[15]

Had he been a more skilled mechanic, he would have been killed. His poor craftsmanship was a happy accident, not unlike the success of the innovations that he made in his early films due to technological limitations.

As he convalesced, Lucas reevaluated his life, deciding that perhaps car racing was not in his future. He quickly decided to continue school with the ever-looming Vietnam War on the horizon, a time when teenagers who were not in school were particularly vulnerable to the draft.

After graduation, Lucas enrolled at Modesto Junior College, where he pursued an associate of arts degree, taking a particular interest in sociology and anthropology. There he became interested in anthropological rituals of love, a subject that would inform his first successful film, *American Graffiti*. *American Graffiti* focused on 1950s car culture as integral to the mating rituals among West Coast teens. Lucas was interested in unraveling the mysteries of sex and dating and finding out why he was having so much difficulty in these areas. He graduated from Modesto Junior College in 1964, winding up with a two-year associate's degree.

While he no longer had designs on racing cars professionally, Lucas had not given up on cars completely. He still spent time around the race circuits and talked with old friends like Allen Grant. He started bringing around an 8 mm movie camera that his father had given him. He met cinematographer Haskell Wexler through Grant, who asked Lucas to help Wexler with a car problem. When Wexler and Lucas met and the younger man said he was interested in film, Wexler suggested he try to get into the University of Southern California.

Before Lucas applied to USC along with Plummer, he expressed an interest in applying for art school at the Art Center College of Design in Pasadena to study illustration and photography. Once his old man caught wind of his son's interest in attending art school, the elder Lucas squashed George's plans by refusing to pay the tuition and declaring that there would be no artists in the Lucas family.[16] USC, on the other hand, was a well-known university in the area and more to the conservative patriarch's liking.

Following his associate's degree, Lucas began film school at USC in 1964 as a junior. According to Lucas, the film students "were kind of the geeks and nerds of our era. For many, it was the first time they'd had a clique of their own, or a gathering place where they could talk about their interests—film—without sniggering or eye-rolling from the cool kids."[17] Lucas viewed much of his life through the dichotomous prism of nerd versus cool, seemingly always coming out on the side of the former.

Even among oddballs, Lucas cut an odd figure during his first year at USC. According to his roommate Randy Epstein, Lucas looked as though he packed clothes that he thought Californians might wear based on movies that he had seen. Don Glut said that Lucas looked very conservative, like an aspiring businessman. Hal Barwood noted that Lucas resembled Buddy Holly. Lucas acted very nervous and was silent for long periods of time. When he did talk, his voice sounded like Kermit the Frog from the Muppets.[18] Lucas's isolation would manifest in his first films at USC, which he called "tone poems" that featured very little human interaction, dialogue, or plot. They suggested an existential worldview, curious, paranoid, and sad.

At film school, Lucas was a dork among dorks, a standout dork. The film-school fraternity Delta Kappa Alpha initially rejected him because he was such a dork. Once the organization finally approved him, he shunned them, a sign of things to come with his own fandom. Even though sex was typically a major part of college life, Lucas did not socialize much at all, especially with women. His buddy John Milius, a fellow USC student who eventually wrote the screenplays for such films as *Dirty Harry*, *Apocalypse Now*, and *Red Dawn*, noted that "George was chasing girls. . . . He didn't catch them, but he *was* chasing them." Another buddy and fellow film student at USC, Richard Walter, was even more definitive: "I've read books that claimed George was a ladies' man. It's nonsense. He was very, very reticent." Epstein's girlfriend once set up George with one of her girlfriends. For many weeks, George only talked to the girl on the phone. Over many hours, he asked her to describe herself. Based solely on her descriptions, Lucas, to her horror, created and presented her with a full-scale oil portrait.[19]

After his first year at USC, Lucas contracted mononucleosis. Despite the disease being known as the kissing disease, all of his buddies knew that George had not contracted the disease from kissing but rather from stress, since everyone knew that George was not getting any action.

By his second year of film school, Lucas had grown a beard and ditched most of his square threads. The beard in particular marked him as an honorary radical, deservedly or not. He also began to make a name for himself as the best student in the entire class. He worked harder than everyone else and began getting into French New Wave filmmakers like François Truffaut and Jean-Luc Godard, extraordinarily cool filmmakers with equally cool films. Truffaut and Godard were former film critics turned filmmakers who created tough, sexy, personal films. Like the American New Wave of the 1970s that emerged as a dramatic alternative to the American studio system, the French New Wave was a direct critical response to the French filmmaking establishment, which emphasized craft over innovation and privileged known filmmakers over newcomers. Two films that captured the French New Wave zeitgeist were Truffaut's 1959 film *The 400 Blows* and Godard's 1960 film *Breathless*. Both films were shot documentary-style on location with tight budgets and low levels of natural light, featuring a cast and crew largely drawn from family and friends of the filmmakers. Truffaut and Godard employed innovative editing methods such as long uninterrupted scenes, jump cuts, and fragmentation. The style was a new mix of meta-filmmaking, simultaneously drawing attention to the filmmaking process and to the film itself as artifice, and documentary realism, while presenting a fictive story. Both stories also featured alienated anti-hero protagonists who are punished for thumbing their noses at the contemporary world and for their nonconformity. *The 400 Blows*, in particular, might be thought of as a French version of *The Catcher in the Rye* as it features a schoolboy at odds with a menacing culture and society that he does not understand and eventually rejects.

Many of the young American filmmakers of this era did not even like American films. They preferred foreign films: Kurosawa and the French New Wave, including Truffaut and Godard. These filmmakers came of age when revolutions peppered the air. They thought of themselves in that light and could be found at drive-ins watching B-films by Roger Corman or in art houses that screened foreign films by Fellini and Bergman.

Lucas earned a reputation for high production value in part, according to some of his classmates, because if he needed money—to get an aerial shot by renting an airplane, for example—he could count on his old man to pony up the quick cash. He was still the kid on the block with the cool toys, capitalizing on his financial power. Lucas's ability to procure cash as a film student at USC was another example of his relationship with money, his upper-middle-class family, and savvy business sense.

Lucas quickly distinguished himself as a rebel who was not afraid to break the rules, and as a budding film genius. He was interested in the French movement *cinema verité*, or truth cinema, a documentary style of filmmaking that focused on real people in real situations. He considered himself an avant-garde filmmaker and even thought of dropping his first name.[20] Lucas and his band of merry pranksters broke into the film editing rooms in order to use the editing machines at night. He used color film when he was not supposed to, edited in music when he was not supposed to, and generally did whatever he wanted to. His feeling was that as long as he made good films, the rules were of no concern to him.[21]

Lucas's transition from hot-rodder to filmmaker and his growing impulse to take creative control of his projects took shape during his experience in the vaunted USC film school course Cinema 480, offered during his final semester. The instructor, Douglass Cox, divided the class into film crews. Not everyone would be able to work in the role of their choosing. Not everyone could be the director, the writer, or the editor. In Lucas's case, he wound up being the writer as well as the director.

Lucas took his crew to Willow Springs Race Track near Rosamond, California, where racer Peter Brock paced his yellow Lotus 23. Lucas filmed the driver racing against time from all angles, including from the driver's perspective, an aerial perspective, from long range, and a one shot of the timekeeper. Sometimes the car would barely be the focus of the film as it zoomed in and out of the shot. Brock's best lap time was 1:42.08, which wound up being the name of Lucas's film. Similar to his later film *American Graffiti*, in *1:42.08*, the camera lovingly lingers over the cars as the engines roar and rise and fall like a breathing body. There is virtually no dialogue in the film. The film communicates through quick cuts that simulate confusion and danger. At one point, the racecar spins out of control. In addition to the lack of dialogue, there is not much of a plot either. However, the film manages to convey a vison of hypermasculinity, of danger, of the possibilities and limitations of machines handled by driven men.

Lucas called the film a visual tone poem and delivered the project on time. The film played to Lucas's strengths and masked his weaknesses. He did not have to write any dialogue. The film presented a man and his machine under total control by the director.[22] Lucas already displayed a penchant for technology over humanity, a recurring theme in his films and in his life.

Lucas's insecurity about his own writing partly drove him early on to privilege the role of the director. Lucas once admitted, "I was always terrible in English . . . I think I'm a *terrible* writer . . . I struggled through English classes . . . I did terrible in script writing. I hated stories, and I hated plot, and I wanted to make visual films that had nothing to do with telling a story."[23] Lucas's insecurities regarding his own writing affected the way he told stories. His early work was almost completely devoid of character and plot.

At USC, Lucas developed his ideas about what it meant to be a filmmaker. Lucas noted, "It is a director's medium, there's no getting around that. The writer provides a very important element, but the final product is ultimately left in the hands of the director."[24] The auteur theory of filmmaking asserted that the director of a film is like the author of a book, the driving creative force and the one who should be credited for a great film. This theory is questionable if only because filmmaking, unlike literature, requires many people vitally contributing in important ways. Nevertheless, Lucas bought into the idea early on in his career.

The auteur theory of filmmaking also circumscribes the filmmaker into the unsustainable role of taking sole responsibility for a project. To be thought of as the sole creator of a filmic world is a lot of weight to bear. Lucas later admitted that his time at USC cultivated the feeling that he was a do-it-yourself auteur: "I came out of film school, so I really was a *filmmaker—which means doing it all*

. . . I did everything. I think of myself as a filmmaker still."[25] Lucas's experiences at USC groomed him to be a creator of worlds.

Lucas was the rebel student against the academic empire. He quickly earned a reputation as a genius in melding different technologies and graphic images. He scoffed at the idea that he or any other student needed to help weaker film students. To Lucas, it was a competition to get the film in the can, and a student who did not have what it took should not have been there in the first place.

Lucas graduated from USC with a bachelor's degree in filmmaking on August 6, 1966. He was available for the draft and tried to enlist. He reported for his physical but was rated 4-F and failed because doctors diagnosed him with diabetes. Lucas's failure to get into the military was another hit to his already deeply wounded masculinity, shot through from childhood bullying and sexual failure. His diabetes diagnosis was significant because it prevented him from indulging in drugs and alcohol like many of his soon-to-be filmmaking contemporaries composing the American New Wave. Diabetes kept his shoelaces straight and his nerd persona intact.

Not long after graduating, Lucas met his future wife, Marcia Griffin. Verna Fields hired them both to help create a film about Lyndon B. Johnson's overseas tours. Marcia Griffin had endured a hard-knock life compared to the relatively pampered Lucas. She and her sisters grew up on several air force bases until her father abandoned the whole family. She was always interested in movies, and after dropping out of night school where she studied chemistry, Sandler Films hired her as an apprentice film librarian after which she began a film editing apprenticeship required by the Motion Picture Editor's Guild to get a union card. Despite her challenging upbringing, Marcia had the look of a sophisticate. In fact, she was born in Modesto just like Lucas while her father was stationed at nearby Stockton.[26]

According to Marcia, George was the intellectual, and she was the vapid valley girl. They argued a lot while working on the Lyndon B. Johnson film, but George appreciated that Marcia would not let him walk all over her. Marcia Griffin was a terrific editor. According to John Milius, she was the best editor that he had ever worked with. She had an innate ability to take a film and make it better. Her arrangement instincts were totally on point.

When Lucas met Marcia, who was a year younger and even shorter than he was, she made it clear that she looked down on students. She was also extremely cute, well out of Lucas's league. John Milius said of the pair, "We all wondered how little George got this great looking girl."[27] Despite the unlikely pairing, the two soon moved in together. The general reaction was astonishment that such an attractive and intelligent woman could see anything in a nerd like Lucas, however talented he might be.

It was clear to Marcia that Lucas was a very thoughtful and able filmmaker, and that he treated film with reverence. Lucas was no longer the wimpy kid lacking in confidence and hiding behind older boys or men whom he revered. It was his talents as a filmmaker that won Marcia over.

Although he had no specific plans after college, Lucas assumed that he would become a documentary filmmaker. At that time, it was very difficult for anyone not already affiliated with Hollywood by way of family connections to get into Hollywood, even as a low-level assistant. Many young, newly graduated filmmakers simply grew disillusioned with the difficulty of breaking into Hollywood and pursued something else.

Lucas returned to USC in January 1967 as a graduate student. He spent his days in class and his afternoons cutting film for Verna Fields, with Marcia by his side. He spent many of his nights as a teaching assistant for cinematography instructor Gene Peterson. Lucas's students in that particular class were military cameramen from the navy and air force. It was his job to get these servicemen to loosen up a bit in their techniques. They shot by the book, and Lucas was supposed to teach them how to use available light and to think about form and composition, to think more like artists than servicemen. It was sort of an odd situation for Lucas, given that the Vietnam War was on the front page of the newspapers nearly every day and sentiments about the war and returning servicemen were generally negative. Yet here he was, teaching a room full of straightlaced GIs. He certainly was not the figure of a sixties radical by the standards of his contemporaries.

Lucas, always the opportunist, realized that because the military sponsored the class, the available equipment would be beyond that of a regular USC class—even a graduate class—and would likely include unlimited access to color film and sound. Lucas also shrewdly realized that the men themselves would be adept at taking orders. Lucas saw this as an opportunity to make a film. He already had an idea for a longer film about a man running from the police in a repressive police state.[28] One challenge was that these navy students, many of whom were twice as old and twice as large as the scrawny man with a goatee who introduced himself as their instructor for the coming spring semester, displayed outright hostility toward Lucas.

Realizing that some of his students were not interested in taking orders from a civilian with a beard, Lucas divided the class into two film crews, with the goal of making a film just like his professor did in his Cinema 480 course. The two teams would compete. Lucas would lead one team, and the ranking officer would lead the other. He planned to make a big brother escape film, a futuristic visual film with no major characters or dialogue, a film that hid his lack of writing skills.

He and his crew shot the film over three long days in January 1967, running themselves ragged. Lucas spent the next several weeks editing the film with Marcia. He titled it *Electronic Labyrinth THX 1138 4EB*. It was a fifteen-minute short that he would turn into his first feature film four years later. Both the fifteen-minute USC film and the feature film were by all accounts avant-garde films that looked like nothing else.

The film imagines life in the twenty-fifth century driven by dehumanizing technical production and loveless and sexless relationships, a plot that could be applied to the rest of Lucas's life. It begins with a visually distorted screen and a column of numbers to the left, featuring a woman with a number on her forehead saying that she is not in love but has the ideal mate. Printouts of digits and strange mechanical ambient sounds of tinny voices dominate the film until a man with 1138 written on his forehead runs down white institutional hallways as disembodied mechanical voices communicate on a scanner. It becomes clear that the subject, 1138, is trying to escape this hellish world. At one point a piercing noise stops him in his tracks, reminiscent of the 1961 Kurt Vonnegut story "Harrison Bergeron" in which characters are tortured by piercing noises that interrupt their ability to think clearly. Like *1:42.08*, *Electronic Labyrinth THX 1138 4EB* is extremely light on dialogue and plot; machines controlled by men dominate the action. Eventually, THX escapes to what appears to be an above-ground world similar to our own. He is then shown running toward a setting sun. Back in the underground world, a deep, almost godlike voice announces that THX has destroyed himself.

Though similar thematically and stylistically, Lucas's student film is very different from what would become his first feature film. Very little if any of the student film made its way into the feature. However, in both films the subject intends to escape the sepulchral and completely dehumanized world where everything is controlled and love is prearranged based on stated preferences. Lucas was grappling with issues related to love and sex and the social construction of human relationships and mating, an interest that formally began at Modesto Junior College and would later find expression in his film *American Graffiti*. The film is full of paranoia and foreboding, a sort of dystopic nightmare vision of a world without free will and driven toward forced and loveless relationships. The antiseptic film is paradoxically very personal and very cagey at the same time. At twenty-three, Lucas was expressing much fear and paranoia. That the only dialogue in the film seems to be connected to forced relationships suggests that Lucas's fear and paranoia were related to romantic relationships.

*Electronic Labyrinth THX 1138 4EB* was a huge hit. Students cheered from the moment the USC logo appeared on the screen, and the reaction only increased from there. Lucas screened the film for his old man at a film festival. His father, noticing the buzz of the audience and the obviously positive reaction to the film, told George's mother on their way home, "I think we put our money on the right horse."[29] Lucas also showed the fifteen-minute film to Irvin Kershner, who had returned to USC to teach direction. Kershner agreed that the film was very impressive, especially since a student at USC produced it.[30] Others took notice as well, including *Los Angeles Times* film critic Charles Champlin, who agreed that Lucas was someone to watch. Ned Tanen, then a production executive at Universal Studios, made a note to himself to find out who the filmmaker was and to keep an eye on him.[31]

The highest honor Lucas's student film received prior to it being optioned for a feature film was its selection as the best dramatic film at the third National Student Film Festival, held in Royce Hall at the University of California, Los Angeles. Sitting in the audience during the film screening was a twenty-three-year-old junior from Cal State Long Beach named Steven Spielberg. Spielberg said about the film,

> I didn't know ahead of time about any of the films . . . so I anticipated nothing. . . . I saw a number of shorts first—but when *THX* came on, there was so much virtuosity in the craft and the vision and the emotion of that story that . . . I couldn't believe it was a student film. . . . It absolutely stopped the festival. You could have heard a pin drop in the theater. . . . My first impression was I hate you! . . . I hate that guy, man! He's so much better than I am![32]

Spielberg's response was indicative of an era that was competitive and ego driven. Directors often thought of themselves in relation to other men and their successes not only with films but also with money and women. In filmmaking prowess, Lucas could compete with anyone.

Feeling invigorated and empowered, Lucas applied for a prestigious scholarship opportunity with Columbia Pictures. Writer/producer Carl Foreman, who was overseeing production on the Gregory Peck film *Mackenna's Gold*, offered four students the opportunity to come to the set of the film and observe the film crew and produce their own short films that could be used promotionally later on.

Once Lucas arrived at the Arizona desert and realized that the scholarship was not for making his own film but for ultimately promoting *Mackenna's Gold*, he quickly went off on his own in direct defiance of Foreman and created another tone poem called *6–18–67*, capturing the existential life of the Arizona desert.[33] All the money at Foreman's disposal on the set struck Lucas to his core. He noted, "It was mind-boggling to us because we had been making films for three hundred dollars, and seeing this incredible waste—that was the worst of Hollywood."[34] The scholarship offered Lucas and the other filmmakers all the equipment they needed, including cameras, lighting, and film, as well as $150 a week. Lucas lived on $25 a week and saved $800.

Although Foreman was not impressed at the time with Lucas's tone poem about the desert, he later reluctantly admitted that Lucas's *6-18-67*, eventually shown on Los Angeles PBS, actually did make a statement. The film has even less of a plot than *1:42.08* and fewer human beings. There is an existential quality to the film, however, as it documents a day in the desert, beginning with a sunrise and ending with a sunset. Lucas's desert is oddly full of life as birds chirp in the wind and small animals that look like little chipmunks nervously skitter about. The cuts are quick, and the camera moves in and out of focus on flowers, with noisy cars rushing by. The trajectory of the film moves from the wild to human-made tools and artifacts. After images of a metal structure and windmill, Lucas centers the camera on grazing sheep that bleat and move about. One cannot miss the misanthropic point, likening humans in the desert to sheep. Eventually the camera captures men on horseback and then a couple of quick shots of the camera crew and the production team for *Mackenna's Gold*. Amidst the shots of the desert landscape, the film production appears rickety and temporary. After the shots of the production crews and a bit of dialogue, there is a fast-motion sequence of the clouds, suggesting that once humans have intervened, the natural world speeds up toward an inevitable decline. Shortly after the fast-motion sequence, there is a storm. After the storm, the sun sets and the film is over. The message in the film seems to be that human intervention in nature is both destructive and fleeting and perhaps just another part of the cycle of life. There is a clear and lamentable movement in the film from the natural world to the mechanical world. Lucas's preoccupation with the perversion of the natural world by the mechanical would dominate his stories as well as his own life.

*Mackenna's Gold* is a western starring Gregory Peck about men pursuing gold and the promise of wealth. The western genre has always been a vehicle for American masculinity, positing that men achieve a sense of themselves as men by constantly pursuing riches and women. Even though Lucas eschewed the film in order to work on a more personal tone poem or meditation about the desert and the existential nature of life, he was also in pursuit of gold—if not women—just like Mackenna and the boys.

Upon returning from his work on *Mackenna's Gold*, Lucas found out that his USC professors had nominated him and Walter Murch for the Samuel Warner Memorial Scholarship, which awarded the winner an opportunity to work at the Warner Bros. studios for six months in any department with a stipend of $80 a week. If nothing else, it was a shot at breaking into the studio system. Lucas and Murch made a pact that whoever won would use the experience to help the other. Lucas won and made good on his promise years later by hiring Murch to create the sound for *American Graffiti*.

As Lucas found out, the studios were dying. The old model of big-budget studio filmmaking was on the way out, and the big moguls of old were dying off. This was a pivotal moment in filmmaking history and one on which Lucas would capitalize. Little did he know that he would first help nearly destroy the studio system and then have a hand in making it stronger than ever.

An apprentice system that privileged the sons of union members dominated the old studio system. These men were often the last hired and first to be fired. Daily operations in the 1950s were still in the hands of the pre-war generation of producers, directors, department heads, and crews who were in their fifties, sixties, and seventies. In this system, the producer was the man in charge, and everyone else was simply there to do a job. United Artists was the only studio that empowered directors from its inception. Founded by Charlie Chaplin, Douglas Fairbanks, Mary Pickford, and D. W. Griffith, the group wanted directors to be able to control their own destinies and cut out the intermediaries and moguls who got rich off the filmmaker's labor. Sadly, by the end of the 1940s, the company was losing $100,000 a week. In 1951, the company was sold.

Soon the courts ruled that the studios enjoyed an unfair monopoly over theater chains and held too much power when it came to contractual obligations with actors. It became clear that the overhead costs of back lots, wardrobe departments, props, and contracted actors were unsustainable, and the only way for a studio to be financially viable was to focus on financing and distribution rather than production. United Artists, for example, under new ownership, did not even own the films they financed but rather leased them from the producers for seven years. Consequently, they were able to offer directors, actors, and others more artistic freedom and higher profits. This proved to be a winning equation, and UA thrived in the 1960s. Even still, it was difficult for newcomers to break into the industry. The system was extremely nepotistic, whether one was interested in working with costumes or distribution. It was especially hard for directors. Studios almost never gave first-time directors a shot. The studios were not into taking risks with inexperienced directors and uninterested in providing the needed experience.

Weakened by court rulings as well as the emergence of television as an alternative medium for entertainment, the old men who ran the studios were also increasingly out of touch with the kids coming of age in the 1950s and 1960s. The studios were still churning out big-budget movies and expensive musicals featuring Doris Day and Rock Hudson. By the late sixties, the studios were all in terrible financial shape.

The Warner Bros. studio was nearly a ghost town of inactivity. *Finian's Rainbow* starring Fred Astaire, another remnant of the old studios, was the only movie production on one lot. Soon the director of the film, twenty-eight-year-old Francis Ford Coppola, noticed a skinny little USC student watching his production and walked up to him and said, "See anything interesting?" To which Lucas replied, "Nope. Not yet."[35]

## 2

# THESE AREN'T THE DROIDS YOU'RE LOOKING FOR

From 1967 to 1972, a flurry of films by a group of fresh-faced, newly minted maverick directors ignited what the press soon began calling the "New Hollywood." Beginning with *Bonnie and Clyde* and *The Graduate* in 1967; *2001: A Space Odyssey* and *Rosemary's Baby* in 1968; *The Wild Bunch*, *Midnight Cowboy*, and *Easy Rider* in 1969; *M\*A\*S\*H* and *Five Easy Pieces* in 1970; *The French Connection*, *Carnal Knowledge*, *The Last Picture Show*, and *McCabe & Mrs. Miller* in 1971; and finally *The Godfather* in 1972, what distinguished the creators of these films was their unapologetic belief in themselves as artists compared to the studio directors of old Hollywood, who had little power and merely thought of themselves as hired guns. In the New Hollywood, the role of the director as the chief creative force behind a film differed from the on-set hierarchy in the studio system of the 1930s and 1940s. In that era, the producer was the only member of the film crew who worked on a film from beginning to end. The director mostly handled the actors and left the set once principal shooting was over. They were low in the power structure of the film, only slightly above the writers.

The 1970s was the decade of auteurism and the American director who defined his work through voice and style, drawing on personal stories more like a poet or fiction writer. These directors strove to create personal styles and filmic brands that distinguished them from their contemporaries. These men included Peter Bogdanovich, Francis Ford Coppola, Warren Beatty, Stanley Kubrick, Dennis Hopper, Mike Nichols, Woody Allen, Bob Fosse, Robert Benton, Arthur Penn, John Cassavetes, Alan Pakula, Paul Mazursky, Bob Rafelson, Hal Ashby, William Friedkin, Robert Altman, and Richard Lester. Then later,

Martin Scorsese, Steven Spielberg, George Lucas, John Milius, Paul Schrader, Brian De Palma, and Terrence Malick.[1]

Auteurism was a French New Wave term employed by Andrew Sarris in the *Village Voice* newspaper as a way of assessing filmmakers and making sense of their films, an academic system of analysis helpful in discussing filmmakers and films in relation to directorial vision.[2] The implicit assumption in auteurism was that individual directors made unique films. For some, the American New Wave marked a golden age and "the last great time."[3] For others, the era did not quite live up to its potential, similar to the way the Harlem Renaissance has often been described as an important historic era that ended all too quickly. Instead of support drying up from white patrons due to economic disaster, the demise of the New Hollywood has often been unfairly blamed on George Lucas and Stephen Spielberg for introducing the blockbuster popcorn flick and ruining American audiences' taste for serious films.

Control and power were key ingredients in the New Hollywood as vast amounts of never-before-seen money changed hands. There was a paradoxical process at play where the directors, most of whom were friends or acquaintances, collaborated and shared their work but at the same time were intensely competitive. As Scorcese noted, "There was always a fine line, where maybe one person was getting more attention than the other. But if the person who's getting less attention sees your rough cut, he could steer you in a negative way on purpose. Without even realizing it. Because of the jealousy."[4] When Brian De Palma saw an early cut of Scorcese's film *Mean Streets*, jealousy drove him disingenuously to urge Scorcese to cut one of the best scenes in the film, a scene where De Niro and Keitel improvise in the back room of a club. Scorcese took his advice and took the scene out, only to reinsert it in a later round of edits.

An odd tension between artistic integrity and making money infected everything. Filmmakers wanted it both ways, and for a time they were able to have it both ways. They were able to make the kinds of films they wanted to make while enjoying financial and critical success. If a film did not make money, it was often defended as too out of the mainstream for regular moviegoers, too avant-garde, and yet this apology did not alleviate the resulting feelings of rejection and bruised ego on the part of the director of the financially unsuccessful film.[5] The vast amounts of money at stake eventually undermined the collaborative and fraternal spirit and caused filmmakers to silo themselves off from one another in order to ensure a piece of the pie for themselves.

A hypermasculine virulence necessary for its existence was baked into the New Hollywood era but would also one day kill it. There was too much money, too much jealousy, too much insecurity, and too much greed. These baser qualities trumped the creativity responsible for the movement in the first place. Toxic masculinity defined the era as most, if not all, the primary directors were men, all competing for the same goals of fortune and fame like cowboys on the prairie in pursuit of gold. Rampant alcohol and drug abuse—especially cocaine, which Dennis Hopper claimed his film *Easy Rider* put on the map—was another reason for the relatively short duration of the era.[6] In a *Playboy* article, Jack Nicholson linked the use of cocaine with sex, noting that it helped him with premature ejaculation.[7]

Part of what separated Lucas from his contemporaries was that he was, for the most part, substance-free, largely because he was diabetic. He did not smoke or do drugs. He did not eat sweets, and he very rarely drank. By contrast, Scorsese later admitted that *New York, New York* was such a disaster because he was too strung out on cocaine to make the necessary changes. He felt like he deserved a free pass from the critics because of his earlier films like *Mean Streets* and *Taxi Driver*. He was eventually put on lithium to control his angry and violent outbursts, all the while continuing to indulge in massive amounts of cocaine.[8]

Francis Ford Coppola nearly had a nervous breakdown on the way-over-budget set of *Apocalypse Now*, where the cast and crew worked amidst a constant haze of pot smoke. Martin Sheen famously performed one of his scenes in a hotel room, completely wasted, at the urging of Coppola. Meanwhile, the squeaky-clean Lucas pumped out a parade of hit films one after the other. The culprit for the end of the American New Wave was drugs and ego, as well as a brand of toxic masculinity tied to the auteur theory that undermined the work. Steven Spielberg also avoided drugs, noting, "I never took LSD, mescaline, coke, or anything like that. . . . But I went through the entire drug period, several of my friends were heavily into it. I would sit in a room and watch TV while people climbed the walls."[9]

Lucas and Spielberg were nerds. They were nerds because they did not do drugs and party. They were nerds because they did not chase women. They were nerds because their films were considered science fiction and made a lot of money. Drugs and sex in part defined the era, and Lucas and Spielberg were not a part of that scene.

Spielberg referred to his childhood as the "wimpy years," describing himself as "the weird, skinny kid with acne." Like Lucas, he had a crew cut and large ears, and like Lucas, he was bullied, remembering, "We were all just trying to make it through the year without getting our faces pushed in the drinking fountain."[10] Nevertheless, the era clearly had a huge impact on Lucas and Spielberg, who would have rather been considered gritty, rugged, auteurs than nerdy science fiction filmmakers. The truth was that the whole lot of them were nerds, including De Palma, Scorcese, Coppola, and the rest. They were film geeks who loved one another's company. Lucas and Spielberg were only worse at hiding it.

Within a short time at the Warner Bros. lot on the set of *Finian's Rainbow*, Coppola hired Lucas to be his administrative assistant for $3000 for six months' work. Coppola challenged Lucas to come up with at least one brilliant idea every day. Lucas did not disappoint. Coppola also challenged Lucas to begin working on a screenplay, admonishing him that a director needed to also write. When Coppola wrapped for *Finian's Rainbow* in the fall of 1967, he convinced Lucas to be his right-hand man on his next film, *The Rain People*, for which Coppola was given $750,000 as well as an extra $3000 for Lucas to write the extended script for *THX 1138 3B*. In old footage showing Lucas with Coppola on the set of *The Rain People*, Lucas looks impossibly skinny, with a very narrow face and a shock of wavy black hair curling back in a bedhead bouffant.

Coppola was able to get the deal he wanted for *The Rain People*: to shoot on location away from the studio, essentially on the road and without the studio having script approval.[11] For Coppola and Lucas, the ultimate goal was to make films outside the studio system.

With the success of *Easy Rider* in 1969, the possibility of Lucas and Coppola realizing their dream of making movies independently was within their grasp. Dennis Hopper wrote, directed, and produced *Easy Rider* completely outside the studio system on a small budget of $350,000. The only thing the studio did was distribute the film. *Easy Rider* would go on to be one of the most profitable films of all time and demonstrate to other filmmakers that it could be done. The film features two bikers, Wyatt and Billy, who smuggle a large amount of cocaine from Mexico to Los Angeles and fence it for cash. They celebrate by biking to New Orleans for the Mardi Gras Festival, until a couple of rednecks eventually kill them both. The film operates as a metaphor for the counterculture and its plight against the oppressive dominant culture. *Easy Rider* held a mirror to a culture that had not yet seen itself in film. No one had ever smoked a joint in a film without going out and committing an atrocity until *Easy Rider*.

Lucas viewed the studio system as creatively restrictive and uninspiring. He was interested in toppling the power structure and democratizing the film-making process. Over the years, he made comments reflecting a Marxist ethos in which the central goal was to tie the worker to his or her product. Lucas admitted, "[We] learned one rule that came out of the '60s: Acquire the means of production."[12] Though the success of *Easy Rider* was a wake-up call for the studios as well as for filmmakers, it was hard to believe that anyone thought this style of filmmaking and filmmaker was sustainable or replicable. The success of *Easy Rider* meant that the studios had finally connected with the younger audience. Dennis Hopper was an overnight sensation and a counterculture celebrity, singlehandedly representing the new style of the New Hollywood that contained the seeds of its own demise. Hopper and Fonda were classic renegade filmmakers who seized a moment and bottled the zeitgeist of an era. No one could have been more different from Dennis Hopper than George Lucas, but even Lucas noted, "The studio system is dead. It died. . . . The power is with the people now. The workers have the means of production."[13]

The film production company American Zoetrope represented Coppola's vision to remake the film industry in his own image, a sort of filmmaking commune, totally free from the studio system and housed in a big sprawling mansion with state-of-the-art equipment. Coppola named Lucas executive vice president.

Because Spielberg was working for Universal, Coppola felt like he was part of the studio system and therefore part of the problem rather than the solution. Spielberg offered, "I wasn't really in Francis's circle. I was an outsider, I was the establishment, I was being raised and nurtured at Universal Studios, a very conservative company, and in his eyes, and also in George's eyes, I was working inside the system."[14]

Coppola negotiated a seven-picture deal with Warner Bros. that included $300,000 up front for the development of *THX*. After languishing over many drafts, Lucas finally finished a viable draft of *THX* with the help of Walter Murch, as he had worked with Lucas on the outline for the original student film. Lucas was also casting and scouting locations. Initially he wanted to shoot the film in Japan in order to achieve a futuristic look. Funded by Zoetrope, Lucas visited Japan along with his art director and met with Japanese officials who were excited about the project. Lucas found several great locations, including a power plant, but soon realized that acquiring permits was going to be very difficult, if not impossible. Consequently, Lucas returned to scout the Bay area for locations that might capture the look he wanted.

Lucas began filming *THX 1138* on Monday, September 22, 1969, shooting from 8:00 a.m. to 7:00 p.m. in the still-unfinished Bay Area Rapid Transit system. For the title role, Lucas hired Robert Duvall, whom he had met while shooting Coppola's *The Rain People*. He decided on Duvall even before he finished the script. Lucas completed shooting *THX* on the night of November 21, 1969. After principal photography was complete, he took his film home to Mill Valley where he planned to edit the movie in his attic rather than at Zoetrope. The Zoetrope offices were too busy and noisy, with too many distractions. Working at Zoetrope was like trying to write a novel in a newspaper office. George, his wife Marcia, and Walter Murch spent nearly six months editing the film. George and Marcia worked on the editing by day, and Murch worked on the sound by night. The three would have breakfast and dinner together and discuss how the film was coming along. Lucas loved the way the sound complemented his visuals.

By the spring of 1970, the film was nearly complete. Lucas was very happy with the work the three had done, but Marcia was not so sure. Lucas insisted that *THX* was all about emotion, but Marcia did not think it worked. She was having trouble emotionally engaging with it. She said the film left her feeling cold. This could have also described their marriage based on comments she made to Lucas's friends.[15] The criticism only angered Lucas. He was not willing to see the film from Marcia's point of view, let alone make any changes based on it. Marcia simply accepted her husband's position and continued to edit the film in line with his vision, but she was not very happy about it. Perhaps Marcia was already thinking about leaving Lucas. What had drawn her to the man in the first place was his editing skills, and she was calling those abilities into question. This dynamic would repeat itself in relation to Lucas and his fans. Lucas's relationships seemed to ebb and flow on the waves of his filmmaking successes and failures.

The dystopic nightmare of *THX 1138* carries its message of impending dehumanization by de-emphasizing dialogue and highlighting emotional stress as the protagonist of the film, played by Robert Duvall, encounters nightmarish scenarios from one scene to the next, including being imprisoned in endless white space and nearly being trampled by a stampede of commuting humans. Like many dystopic films, *THX 1138* comments on a world progressing technologically but regressing in humanity. Early in his career, Lucas offered that he was interested in trying to convey emotions through visual techniques rather than through dialogue or traditional narrative.[16]

THX 1138, the handle of the titular protagonist evident on his required badge, and his roommate LUH 3417, played by Maggie McOmie, violate the law by falling in love, having sex, and weening themselves off mandated drugs. Because of the reduced medication, they find themselves unable to function within the highly regulated and controlled world. The state eventually arrests THX and kills his pregnant lover LUH. THX escapes his confinement and desperately makes his way out of the underground fortress to the world above just as the sun is setting. The film is essentially about refusing to accept the way things are. According to Lucas, the idea of setting out into unknown worlds from relative safety is a trope evident in all his films.[17] This trope could also be applied to Lucas's own career as a filmmaker, as Lucas repeatedly cut against the grain.

As will become evident in the story of George Lucas as well as the story of the *Star Wars* franchise, technology has always played a crucial role. From the very beginning, in his early short films at USC, Lucas focused his stories on a culture becoming ever more reliant on technology at the expense of an already flawed humanity. This dynamic would inform almost every aspect of Lucas's life and would be the central concern of the *Star Wars* story, especially as it relates to the Clones, introduced in the prequels, who play a vital role in the destruction of the Jedi.

The sexuality in *THX 1138* is devoid of eroticism and yet plays an important role in the film. In Lucas's world, humans take medication to suppress their sex drive and watch holographic videos of sadistic violence and naked dancing women, such as a bald black woman, a racialized image that recurs in many of Lucas's films. Richard Walter noted, "It [*THX 1138*] manages to have a lot of nudity in it . . . but to be anti-erotic. George's work is extremely non-sexual. He is uncomfortable with sexuality."[18] In the film, the female character LUH takes the initiative and reduces THX's libido-suppressing medication. As a result, the two wind up making love, but the way it looks on camera is anything but sexual. Their bodies are pale, hairless, and joylessly pressed together.

There is also an element of homoeroticism in the film. One obstacle to THX and LUH escaping their hellish situation is that THX's supervisor, SEN 5241, is homosexual and interested in THX as a partner. SEN 5241's roommate is killed for unknown reasons, and, as a result, SEN reprograms the computer so that THX is assigned as his roommate, the implication being that he can enjoy his new roommate as a sexual partner. The state thwarts SEN's plan, arresting and imprisoning him along with THX. In the original screenplay, LUH is captured, raped, and beaten to death on television, but Lucas never shot those scenes.[19] Instead, viewers see that the state has killed LUH and repurposed her name for another developing embryonic human.

*THX 1138* delivers the most overt presentation of sexuality in any of Lucas's films, a sexuality that is hostile and paranoid. LUH manipulates THX into sleeping with her, for which they are arrested and imprisoned. Homosexuality presents itself as an obstacle that can potentially beset the protagonist. Heterosexuality itself is criminalized, and homosexuality manifests as an added peril.

On Thursday, November 19, 1970, Coppola showed up at Warner Bros. to present the final cut of Lucas's film. The executives hated it, and the day became known as "Black Thursday" among those involved with Coppola's production company Zoetrope. The executives at Warner promised to release *THX* with the stipulation that the seven-picture deal with Zoetrope was officially over, and they wanted their $300,000 back. The studio's shortsighted reaction cost them the rights to the films *Apocalypse Now* and *The Conversation*, among many other classic 1970s American films.

Coppola had to tell George that Warner Bros. intended to give his movie to one of their in-house editors for cuts. Warner editor Rudi Fehr cut four minutes from the film. Lucas was embarrassed as well as angry. Warner finally released the film in March 1971. That *THX* ruined it for five other filmmakers and their deals with Coppola's Zoetrope was humiliating and deeply wounding for Lucas and set him on a path to *Star Wars*.

Ever since Lucas and Coppola saw independent filmmaker John Korty's personal filmmaking studio in his barn on Stinson Beach in 1970, the two friends wanted something similar for themselves. Coppola nearly achieved it with American Zoetrope, housed in a three-story loft in a warehouse in San Francisco. The next year—1971—Lucas created his own independent film company and called it Lucasfilm Ltd.

The lukewarm reception of *THX* devastated Lucas. The general feeling was that he was a cold fish, science fiction type of director who had trouble connecting with a mainstream audience. Lucas heard the same criticisms from Marcia, not only about his films but also about his abilities as a lover. Lucas responded by pleading, "I do have emotions, and I'm not a weird sci-fi guy."[20] One can hear in these lamentations, "I'm not a nerd! I'm not a nerd!" In order to prove that he could connect with mainstream audiences, Lucas began working on his next film, *American Graffiti*, almost immediately. He would experience another embarrassment when nearly two years later *American Graffiti* suffered the exact same treatment as *THX*, a form of corporate bullying that set Lucas on the path to film mogul and lord of his own empire.

Lucas first pitched his eighteen-page proposal for *American Graffiti* to David Picker at United Artists, who offered him $10,000 to develop the script. With the money, he hired an old USC film school classmate, Richard Walter, to write a draft of the script. Lucas did not like Walter's script at all. Part of the problem with Walter's version of the script was that it was too sexual. Walter himself agreed that he had a lot of sex in the script but noted that "[Hey], it's adolescence! Though not, I gather, George's adolescence."[21] Over a three-week period in 1971, Lucas wrote the screenplay himself from 8:00 a.m. until 8:00 p.m., seven days a week. Once he was finished, he sent the completed script to Picker at UA, who rejected it outright.

Lucas then showed up at Ned Tanen's office at Universal in early 1972, armed with a cassette tape filled with music that he wanted to use for the film. He pitched the film to Tanen as a musical. Tanen, who had already read Lucas's version of the script and was a car guy, got what Lucas was trying to do and offered him a $750,000 budget. Lucas began pre-production immediately and would complete filming of *American Graffiti* on August 4 of that same year. The

1950s lovefest would not last. He sent a completed version of the film to Universal in December, and the studio was wary of its chances for mainstream success.

By January 1973, Universal executives were still not confident about the film and sent Tanen to San Francisco for a public screening. Despite a tremendous response from the audience, who seemed to love the film, Tanen thought the movie failed. Coppola, while still in the theater, dramatically pulled out his checkbook and offered to buy the film from Universal right then and there. As Warner did with *THX*, Universal handed the film off to their in-house editors, who once again cut four minutes from the film. Lucas was out of his mind with anger.[22]

*American Graffiti*, and in particular the character of Toad, provides tremendous insight into George Lucas's life as a teenager growing up in Modesto, California. Lucas was very much concerned with his nerd persona and how it affected his relationships with women and other men. For Lucas, like many men, dangerous pitfalls and traps that had the potential to unmask him plagued the world of adolescence. The entire film concerns Toad avoiding emasculation, something that concerned Lucas his entire life.

Plummer said there were many similarities between Terry the Toad and George. He said George always wanted the stereotypical blonde but never found her. Another possibility was that George wanted people to *think* he wanted the stereotypical blonde.[23] Several other friends of Lucas have noted that Toad is a spot-on portrayal of the director when he was in high school. In the film, Toad has the night of his life, getting the girl and taking part in an epic drag race. Throughout his great night, however, he is pushed around and bullied.

Toad, introduced right away as a nerd, is the very first character shown in *American Graffiti*, cruising into the parking lot of Mel's drive-in on a scooter in a film about cars. He does, however, *get the blonde*, beginning Lucas's habit of using movies to fulfill his own fantasies.

There are other parallels between Lucas's life in Modesto and *American Graffiti*. For example, Lucas was for a time involved with the local Modesto gang, the Faros, also memorialized in the film. The Faros employed Lucas as a stooge to lure members of other gangs into a fight and then confront them with the rest of the Faro gang once the other gang members were isolated.[24] This act of bait and switch also played into George's penchant for getting close with stronger, tougher male figures in order to protect himself.

Another character in the film, Curt, played by Richard Dreyfuss, represents the literary side of Lucas, a sort of romanticized view of himself as a writer. Curt is hardly a nerd at all and signifies a persona that was percolating within George at an early age. Curt, who longs to leave the turkey town of his youth to go to college, gets cold feet the night before he is supposed to fly out to his new college. Curt's character in *American Graffiti*, like Terry, chases a blonde woman, a sort of ghostly apparition played by Suzanne Somers who drives a white T-Bird. Although Somers is certainly a classically beautiful blonde woman, the film celebrates the beauty of the cars as much, or more so, than the women. The "blonde in the T-Bird" and the "Debbie-type" girl easily register to viewers as desirable girls, but the camera lingers sensually on the cars more than the women, not unlike in Lucas's early film, *1:42:08*.

*American Graffiti*, according to Lucas, centers on American dating rituals in the late 1950s and early 1960s; however, the film contains very few if any images of healthy romantic relationships. Lucas depicts women as dangers and obstacles to freedom and success. Terry spends much of the film simply trying to avoid humiliation.

Toward the beginning of the film, Steve offers Toad the use of his car while he is away at college. Toad enthusiastically accepts and immediately invites the first girl he sees to a drive-in movie. Right after he asks the girl out, his older buddy John Milner, a cool and tough hot-rodder, sneaks up behind Toad and pulls down his pants, humiliating him. This scene echoes the story of older boys holding Lucas down, removing his "shoes," and tossing them into the neighboring lawn.

On Toad's first night out in Steve's car, ostensibly "scooping the loop" with the intent of picking up a chick, a man in another car moons Toad, undercutting his confidence. Toad then has an exchange with another man that is full of homosexual innuendo. As the man revs up his engine, Toad asks, "What have you got under there, pal?" to which the man replies, "More than you can handle." Toad dings up Steve's car, and an aggressive, oily used car salesman nearly seduces him. Eventually, Toad sleeps with Debbie but loses Steve's car completely, possibly to theft.

The first time Toad encounters Bob Falfa, played by Harrison Ford, Falfa refers to him as a dork. When Toad and the girl he picks up, Debbie, run into one of her ex-boyfriends, he immediately refers to Toad as a wimp and calls him Einstein. Debbie responds by saying that Toad is very intelligent, even though the film to that point has not demonstrated that Toad has any intelligence at all. Debbie says, "That creep is just horny. That's why I like you. You're different." The salient point here is that Debbie does not think of Toad as a sexual person like the other boys because he is smaller, unathletic, and wears glasses. Problems plague Toad's journey as he desperately tries to assume the role of horny-toad, with mixed results.

Toad eventually pukes his guts out from the booze and his gluttonous foray into the world of men, a world for which he is clearly not cut out. When Toad finally finds Steve's stolen car and attempts to hot-wire it in order to steal it back, two older men jump him and beat him up. The older hot-rodder, John Milner, rescues Toad from his assailants. Toad eventually admits to Debbie that in fact he has no car. To his amazement, Debbie likes him anyway. When she kisses him and agrees to go out with him again, Toad's response is "Ouch." Toad's big coup occurs at the end of the film when he flags a car race between Milner and Bob Falfa.

*American Graffiti* wound up being a smash hit, and Lucas was not shy about taking credit: "I know how good I am," he told the *New York Times*, matter-of-factly. "*Graffiti* is successful because it came entirely from my head. It was *my* concept. And that's the only way I can work."[25] *American Graffiti* ended up on countless best-of lists for 1973 and won a number of awards, including the Golden Globe for Best Musical or Comedy and a New York Film Critics Circle Award for Best Original Screenplay. When Oscar season rolled around, the Academy nominated *American Graffiti* for five Academy Awards, including Best Picture, Director, and Editing. Unfortunately, *Graffiti* lost to *The Sting* in nearly every category.[26]

Although Lucas sensed that there was a New Hollywood on the horizon, he did not try to emulate the New Hollywood style of *Easy Rider*. He recognized that most of what the New Hollywood churned out was pessimistic realism, and he aimed to counter that with life-affirming films that evoked a simpler time. Lucas seemingly learned his lesson, a lesson that Marcia had attempted to teach him while editing his first film, namely that a filmmaker needed to connect emotionally with an audience.

In June 1975, Spielberg released *Jaws*. For other filmmakers of the era, *Jaws* spelled doom for the industry. With *Jaws*, studios realized that opening a film in thousands of theaters and inundating the public with advertising all but ensured sales. The old method was for movies slowly to build a following based on quality. This new way involved studios planning and marketing for the big opening weekend and investing a lot of money up front, which had the effect of making the studios less willing to take on risky films.

Coppola's *The Godfather* marked a turning point for the studios regarding how they released films, as the film was marketed for a year and then released in over 400 theaters nationwide. Coppola's success with *The Godfather* also played a role in Lucas's redemption, in that the studios only agreed to finance *American Graffiti* if Coppola was part of the project. As a result, the success of *American Graffiti* had the opposite effect of *THX* and blew the doors open for young filmmakers. The success of *American Graffiti* paved the way for Scorcese's *Mean Streets* as well as William Friedkin's *The Exorcist*, both hit films.

Spielberg and Lucas wanted to be considered auteurs just like the rest of the filmmakers of the era, maybe even more so since their nerdy personas all but disqualified them, but their successful films had the opposite effect. Instead of enshrining the two successful directors into the 1970s New Hollywood scene, their success had an alienating effect. This would crystallize with the success of Lucas's next film based on his love of *Flash Gordon* serials.

One can think of *Jaws* as a continuation of Roger Corman's drive-in B-movies, only done bigger and better with more money and more skilled people. The aesthetic itself was popcorn blockbuster before there were popcorn blockbuster films. *Jaws* and *Star Wars* marked the ultimate triumph of the B-movie.

The B-film emerged as an attempt by a number of independent theaters to lure audiences back into their theaters at a time of acute economic crisis in the industry during the Great Depression. Along with the double bill, independents introduced lotteries, live acts, quizzes, gifts, and several other gimmicks in order to build up bigger audiences and keep them in their seats a little longer, boosting box office and concession sales while legitimizing increased admission prices. In 1935 MGM and RKO, the last of the majors to adopt double bills in their theaters, announced their decision to screen two features in all but two of their theaters. By 1947, two-thirds of theaters offered double bills. Overproduction by the major studios had accumulated an enormous backlog of unreleased films. It was not until the studios exhausted this reservoir of ready-made second features that it became necessary to set up an entirely new mode of film production, the B unit. Because few theaters could afford the rentals of two top-quality products at the same time, the double bill usually offered a combination of one relatively expensive A-film and one relatively inexpensive B-film. A-film budgets, produced by the major studios throughout the 1940s, typically ranged upwards of $700,000, while B-film budgets ranged below $400,000. In general, the A features' rental was based on a percentage of the box office takings, while the B-films played for a fixed or flat rental and were not so reliant on audience attendance figures. The B units carved out identifiable and distinctive styles for themselves in order to differentiate their product from A productions. In most cases, B units produced films on tight budgets with short shooting schedules, sometimes only a single week. Within these limitations, B units were given much more autonomy than A units controlled by the major studios. Artistic ingenuity in the face of economic intransigence was one commonality among B-films. Initially, B-films were little more than low-budget versions of profitable A releases, but soon this imitative trend was replaced by an oppositional cinematic style that often resulted in great movies that audiences loved.[27] The increased autonomy, limited budgets, and fixed rental fees allowed directors to take risks within subgenres that drove innovation and creativity, qualities possessed by both *Jaws* and *Star Wars*. French critics so influential to the American New Wave taught Americans how to read aspects of their own popular culture. French critics were especially attracted to the B-movie. Low-budget films made quickly by young filmmakers and frequently appearing at the bottom of the ubiquitous double feature provided rich material into which auteur critics could sink their teeth.[28]

As early as 1973, Lucas had a two-page handwritten treatment of something that he called his "Flash Gordon thing" with the tentative title of *The Star Wars*. After King Features declined to sell him the rights to *Flash Gordon*, he decided to create his own characters and set most of the story in space. One of his key visions was a dogfight in space between two spaceships. He often thought of his idea as a superhero in space, a sort of space fantasy.

By the time Lucas pitched *Star Wars* to Universal and asked for a $3 million budget, executives wondered aloud why they should back a $3 million film by an "artsy" director when he already screwed up two films with smaller budgets.[29] This was before Lucas scored a huge hit with *American Graffiti*. Universal wound up declining the film, and Lucas made a deal with 20th Century Fox. Once *American Graffiti* became a big hit, Fox worried that Lucas would demand more money to make *Star Wars*. Instead, Lucas agreed to the original memo, which was not yet a solid contract, with the added stipulation that he would receive merchandising and sequel rights, as well as the right to have his own Lucasfilm produce the movie. The contract would eventually balloon to forty pages, and Lucas would own and control everything, including sequels, television, publishing, and merchandising.[30]

Lucas struggled mightily to write *Star Wars*. Though he would subsequently discount the film, saying that it was a kid's movie and the most conventional film that he could make, he often noted that he bled on the page for nearly three years. His admitted lack of talent when it came to writing forced him to struggle through it. Lucas noted, "You go crazy writing. . . . You get psyched up and go in such strange directions in your mind that it's a wonder that all writers aren't put away someplace."[31]

Marcia and George discussed the fact that during the casting for *Star Wars*, he would be exposed to some of Hollywood's most attractive women, many of whom were rumored to have gotten ahead on their backs, not their talent. They agreed that, should either of them have an extramarital affair, they would confess it to the other. Nothing was further from Lucas's mind. One wonders in retrospect whether Marcia had ulterior motives in laying her cards on the table in relation to possible infidelity. She must have known the chances of Lucas sleeping with another woman were not very strong.

In 1973 and 1974, when George was writing *Star Wars*, Marcia was editing Martin Scorsese's film *Alice Doesn't Live Here Anymore*. Marcia worked on location in Los Angeles and Arizona with Scorsese, and Lucas drove back and forth from San Francisco and Tucson in order to keep an eye on Scorcese and Marcia. *Alice Doesn't Live here Anymore* was the first of Scorsese's films on which Marcia was the lead editor. She also edited his next two films, *Taxi Driver* and *New York, New York*. Marcia made it very clear to her husband that she thought Scorsese was a much more important filmmaker, and that George was wasting his time. She was convinced that *Star Wars* would flop and that George's film would be an embarrassment compared to Scorsese's *New York, New York*, both intellectually and financially. It was not that she thought her husband had no talent; it was just that she thought *Star Wars* was beneath him. She felt strongly that he should be making films that were more artistic, like his contemporaries Coppola and Scorsese. She, like many others, did not believe that what Lucas was doing was even art, let alone avant-garde art. Considering that Marcia's attraction to Lucas by all accounts was in relation to his filmmaking prowess, this was no small matter.[32]

In May 1974, Lucas completed a rough draft of *The Star Wars*. The draft checked in at 191 scenes and over 33,000 words. The protagonist in this draft was a young man named Annikin Starkiller who trains to become a Jedi Bendu with an old general named Luke Skywalker. Two silly droids appear in the manuscript and function as comic relief, as well as a green creature named Han Solo. Additionally, the draft featured a fourteen-year-old princess, a hirsute being called a Wookie, laser-swords, and a general named Darth Vader. The plot at this point included a fight scene in a cantina, a chase through an asteroid belt, a prison rescue, and an awards ceremony. In addition, for the first time, one character bids another goodbye with the words: "May the force of others be with you."

Lucas began casting in August 1974, and several notable actors in Hollywood and New York auditioned for the film, including John Travolta, Nick Nolte, and Tommy Lee Jones. Twenty-three-year old Mark Hamill showed up to audition mostly because his friends talked him into it. Hamill loved science fiction and comic books and was excited about playing the role of a hero in a sci-fi film. Lucas dismissed him not long after he sat down.

For Lucas, finding the right Han Solo proved to be the trickiest task of all. Solo had evolved on the page more than most of the other characters. By the time casting started, the character was no longer a green alien. He was now a world-weary, somewhat cynical pirate, part James Dean, part Humphrey Bogart. It was a role that was going to take just the right amount of swagger and sincerity.

Lucas briefly considered casting an African American, looking closely at twenty-eight-year-old actor Glynn Turman. However, given that he was contemplating a romance between Han and Leia, Lucas was concerned that an interracial relationship might be too distracting for 1970s audiences.[33] That Lucas had in mind an African American at all to play the hypersexual Han Solo is telling, insofar as how he viewed African Americans. For Lucas, like many Americans, African Americans oozed sexuality. It was not the first time Lucas looked to capitalize on the connotative sexuality of African Americans. In *THX 1138*, he used a topless African American woman dancing as an example of hologrammatic porn in his desexualized dystopia. That Lucas decided against casting an African American out of fear of fan reaction is doubly troubling and disappointing.

It was casting director Fred Roos who planted Harrison Ford as a possible actor for the role of Han Solo by hiring him as a carpenter to work at the Zoetrope offices. Ford found acting jobs scarce after his role in *American Graffiti* and returned to carpentry for his primary income. Ford did not want to be in the room working on his knees as a carpenter when there was a casting call; it was too humiliating. "I'm not working a fucking door while Lucas is there," Ford pleaded.[34] Roos suggested to Lucas that Ford read Han's lines with the other actors. Although Lucas was still reluctant to cast anyone from *American Graffiti*, Lucas agreed, and the more Ford read, the more Lucas liked him for the part. Roos's ruse worked.

Mark Hamill had all but forgotten about *Star Wars* when his agent contacted him and told him that Lucas wanted him back for a second audition. Hamill was not confident that he had won the role and was not impressed with Lucas's dialogue. He noted, "There's a line I remember from the original test . . . where I say, 'We can't turn around. Fear is their greatest weapon. I doubt if the actual security there is any greater than it was on Aquilae or Sullust, and what there is, is most likely directed toward a large-scale assault.' And I thought, who talks like this?"[35]

Lucas also invited back Carrie Fisher, the nineteen-year-old daughter of Hollywood actors Debbie Reynolds and Eddie Fisher. She made her acting debut only a year earlier in a small but memorable role in *Shampoo* starring Warren Beatty. Fisher missed the auditions in August, but Roos encouraged Lucas and Fisher to meet. Fisher received her pages of the script, and she too rolled her eyes, though for a different reason—she felt like her character was mostly unconscious, and she wanted more to do in the scenes. Fisher noted, "I got [the part] with the proviso that I went to a fat farm . . . and . . . lose ten pounds."[36]

By the end of 1975, Lucas had been struggling with *Star Wars* for nearly three years, suffering through rejection at the hands of two studios, dealing with skepticism from his friends, a depletion of his savings, and an almost lethal lack of faith from 20th Century Fox. Nevertheless, he was close to finalizing his contract and budget. His cast was falling into place. He scouted locations and reserved sound stages in London. Things looked to be on track to begin filming in March 1976.

There is no indication that Lucas ever intended for Darth Vader to be Anakin Skywalker, or that he would be the father of Luke and Leia, twins separated at birth. While Lucas would, over the course of three decades, perpetuate a kind of retroactive continuity by asserting that this had been his plan all along, in 1975 he still clearly intended for Vader and Luke's father to be separate characters. Vader's backstory, he explained, was about Ben, Luke's father, and Vader, three different characters who were young Jedi knights. Vader kills Luke's father, then Ben and Vader have a confrontation, just as they have in *Star Wars*, and Ben almost kills Vader. As for the name "Vader," Lucas made much of the linguistic coincidence that *vader* is the Dutch word for "father," but it was also a name he likely heard at Downey High School, where he had a schoolmate one grade ahead, an all-conference athlete named Gary Vader. Given Lucas's nerd stature in high school, it seems entirely plausible that he named his first major villain after a jock he loathed in high school.

In January 1976, Lucas was still not happy with the script. Lucas called on Willard Huyck and his wife Gloria Katz, with whom he collaborated on *American Graffiti*, and brought them to London to work on a rewrite. The Huycks worked with their typical speed, sanding some of the jargon-heavy edges off Lucas's script, tightening the dialogue in a few key places, and paying particular attention to the banter between characters, especially the interaction between Han and Leia.

Filming for *Star Wars* began at 6:30 a.m. on Monday, March 22, 1976. It was a catastrophe almost from the start. By the end of the two-week Tunisian shoot, Lucas was desperately unhappy and feeling tremendous pressure and very unsupported by almost everyone involved. On a positive note, Lucas grew quite fond of his actors, especially Mark Hamill, who was exactly his kind of nerd: short, with a geek's gung-ho fondness for comic books and toys. It did not take long for Hamill to realize that Lucas had infused more than a little of himself in the character of Luke. "I'm really playing him in the movie," noted Hamill.[37] Hamill watched Lucas closely as he acted out the scene in which Luke finds a runaway Artoo. Hamill integrated a few of Lucas's quirks—small gestures, quieter dialogue—into his character. Lucas took to warmly calling Hamill "the kid," not unlike Coppola referring to him as "the stinky kid."

Lucas did not want Carrie Fisher looking too feminine. He even forced her to tape down her breasts, noting that there was no jiggling in the Empire. Gary Kurtz had to tell her to tape her breasts because Lucas was too shy to do so.

The British contingent of the film, including Sir Alec Guinness and the British crew at the studio in London, thought the film was complete rubbish and referred to Chewbacca as the dog. Guinness, in particular, told anyone who would listen that he was only interested in the paycheck. Even James Earl Jones, the voice of Darth Vader, refused to have his name appear on the credits, claiming that his contribution was merely special effects and did not require attribution. In this manner, Lucas was still the weakling being bullied by those around him.

On Friday, July 16, 1976, Lucas completed principal photography. Though he ended up twenty days behind schedule, he was very nearly on budget. He was still very upset, though. He did not like the lighting of the film, and he did not like the camerawork. He also started experiencing chest pains. Marcia checked him into a hospital, where doctors diagnosed him with hypertension and exhaustion and ordered him to cut down the stress in his life.

George's inner circle mostly hated early sneak previews of *Star Wars*, including his wife, who told him that his movie was for kids whereas Scorcese's *New York, New York* was for grown-ups, and that nobody was going to take his film seriously.[38] Throughout the process, he made excuses for himself: "This is a Disney movie," he said. "All Disney movies make $16 million, so this picture is going to make $16 million. It cost ten, so we're going to lose money on the release, but I hope to make some of it back on the toys."[39] In retrospect, Lucas's insecure apology that his film was just a Disney movie rings hauntingly prescient. When Lucas showed an early draft of the script to his friends Coppola, Huyck and Katz, and Robbins, none of them were supportive, and all of them thought he should be making more of an artistic statement. George felt horrible and was convinced that he was a failure.[40]

In the 1970s, Lucas counted himself among some of the best young filmmakers of his generation, filmmakers who defined one of the most fertile eras of moviemaking. Almost all of these people at one time or another accused Lucas of not honoring his talent, or selling out, or even ruining the industry. In particular, his wife Marcia ruthlessly criticized Lucas's films, especially *Star Wars* in 1977, comparing it to the much more serious and important films Scorcese made. Spielberg and Lucas were grouped together largely because they were friends but also because they made genre films and did not party like the rest of the filmmakers of the era.

Marcia thought so little of *Star Wars* that in the final stages of editing, she dropped the film to go work on Scorcese's *New York, New York*. Scorcese's editor on the film had died, and in desperation he called Marcia, asking for help. Because Marcia respected Scorcese so much, she came to Marty's aid to the outrage of Lucas, who knew that Scorcese was a party boy and womanizer.

Toward the beginning of 1977, Lucas screened *Star Wars* for a group of friends, including Alan Ladd Jr., Spielberg, Scorcese, Huyck and Katz, Brian De Palma, and *Time* reviewer Jack Cocks. All except Scorcese made it. Some chalked up the director's absence to his fear of flying, but it seemed like there was some sort of issue between him and Lucas. One possible inference was that Lucas was still upset that Marcia had abandoned his film when he needed her most to attend to a man who was clearly out of control. Another possible interpretation is that Marcia and Marty had an affair, and Lucas was upset about it. Regardless, the screening was a disaster. De Palma, in particular, ridiculed Lucas, making fun of the force and interrogating him as to why there was no blood. Among the entire bunch, only Spielberg liked the film—and he loved it.[41]

And so it was amidst all this hate that George and Marcia sat on May 25, 1977, at the Hamburger Hamlet having lunch when they noticed a huge commotion across the street at Mann's Chinese Theatre on Hollywood Boulevard. Lucas recalled it looking like a mob scene, with cops everywhere and lines eight or nine people wide stretching down the street and around the block. After they ate, the two went outside to see what was going on. What was going on was *Star Wars*. Emblazoned on the marquee in big bold letters was *Star Wars*. It was opening day. Later that day, limos dropped off Hugh Hefner and several playboy bunnies who stuck around and watched the film multiple times.[42] To everyone's amazement, nerd culture had triumphed.

Of all the *Star Wars* characters, Han Solo is likely the one whom Lucas most longed to be. It is probably no coincidence that Harrison Ford played both Bob Falfa and Han Solo as alpha-dog males who undermine the nerd protagonists. Like Bob Falfa in *American Graffiti*, Solo is essentially a hot-rodder bad boy, a sort of Disney-fied drug dealer who deals in spices instead of cocaine like the characters in Dennis Hopper's *Easy Rider*. He is a rebel, a lady's man, and embodies the cool. Even his partner Chewie contradistinctively marks Han as a man-who-knows-Indians kind of character like Daniel Boone or Jonah Hex, a characteristic of quintessential American coolness. Solo is reckless but gets away with it; he is thoroughly heroic but reluctant. Han Solo's ship, the Millennium Falcon, is a souped-up spaceship, the fastest in the galaxy due to the modifications that Han and Chewie made themselves.

When Luke and Obi-Wan Kenobi first meet Han and Chewie, Han is surprised that they have not heard of the ship that did the Kessel run in six parsecs. Han notes that despite appearances, the ship had it where it counted, and boasts about his special modifications. Han won the ship from Lando Calrissian in a poker game. Han's "special modifications" are reminiscent of the failed seat-belt modification that saved Lucas's life when he crashed his car into a tree when he was eighteen.

Another character in the *Star Wars* universe that evokes Lucas as a child and young man is Luke Skywalker. His interest in mechanical technology and racing, his inexperience, and his desire for something greater in his life is similar. Like Lucas, he is a nerd. Luke is a whiny ineffectual boy who has a nose for mechanics, not unlike Lucas himself. Luke is far from the Jedi knight that he is fated to become. In his late teens, Luke is ever the greenhorn. His first line in the film regarding his displeasure at having to clean up the droids because he had planned on going to Toshi station to pick up some power converters marks him as a tech geek as well as a whiner. His Uncle Owen, presented as a domineering father figure not unlike George's own father, responds to Luke's rebuke by characterizing his activities as a waste of time. While Luke gives C3PO an oil bath, Luke laments having to stay on Tatooine, referencing Biggs, who has already joined the academy, and paralleling Lucas's own desire to leave Modesto.

Luke's reaction to seeing Leia for the first time as a hologram suggests that he has not had much experience with the opposite sex. He is in awe of her, worshipful, unlike Han Solo later in the film who has no problem verbally sparring with the princess at every turn. The iconic scene of Luke gazing at the two suns of Tatooine foreshadows his fate to move among the stars and transcend his provincial life on Tatooine, even though the first time Luke sets off on his own, he is nearly killed by Tuscan Raiders. If not for Obi-Wan, he would have been killed by the sand people, proving his callowness. Evazan and Ponda bully Luke before Obi-Wan steps in again and cuts Evazan's arm off. Luke is treated like a greenhorn, a sort of sexless little brother or nerdy sidekick, even though he is one of the most important men in the galaxy.

Upon finding Leia in her cellblock, the first thing she says to Luke is that he is a little short to be an Imperial Stormtrooper. Han, on the other hand, is the better pilot and, presumably, the better lover. Once they escape, Luke takes a backseat to Han when bantering with the princess. Luke's one moment of romantic heroism occurs when he swings across the elevator shaft with Leia in an homage to the swashbuckling pirate movies of Lucas's youth. Bob Falfa and Han Solo, both characters played by Harrison Ford, emasculate Terry the Toad and Luke Skywalker.

George Lucas was still incredulous about the popularity of his "Flash Gordon thing." *Star Wars* was selling out at each of the thirty-two theaters in which it was playing, and lines were snaking around the block even for the approaching-midnight shows. Yet Lucas was still unsure. He told Ladd that science fiction films often enjoyed strong opening weekends because of hard-core fans and then dropped precipitously after that. After a little over twenty-four hours, the film had broken attendance records for the highest-ever midweek opening of any film. By the end of 1977, *Star Wars* would officially become the highest-grossing film of all time.

As *Star Wars* was selling out like crazy, Lucas and Marcia traveled to New York for the premier of Scorsese's film *New York, New York*. It was a mess and would go on to be a huge flop. Scorsese blamed his movie's failure on *Star Wars*, noting bitterly that *Star Wars* had taken all the chips off the table, a charge that he would level again four decades later. Scorsese then spiraled further into drugs and depression, while Lucas almost immediately began working on *The Empire Strikes Back*.[43]

The following April, Lucas took his wife to the Academy Awards where *Star Wars* was nominated in ten categories. Marcia took home an Oscar for editing, even though she abandoned the film and her husband to assist Scorsese. *Star Wars* swept nearly every technical award, including art direction, music, visual effects, and editing. Lucas may not have received any awards by name, but in actuality, all the awards were his.

The truth was that Lucas was every bit as great as the other filmmakers of the era. His desire to destroy the studio system marked him as an avant-garde filmmaker. Further, *Star Wars* itself was new and cutting-edge. While it had a more traditional narrative than *THX 1138*, it employed effects and tropes that changed the genre of science fiction and space fantasy forever. It just so happened that the qualities that marked Lucas as an avant-garde filmmaker also marked him as a nerd.

Lucas had always been considered an experimental, artsy, and even hostile and stubborn filmmaker with tremendous film editing skills. Part of what made Lucas such an avant-garde filmmaker was his refusal to accept the way the studio system made movies. He felt as though studio executives generally had no idea what they were talking about and knew very little about film. After *THX 1138* and *American Graffiti* each suffered four minutes of cuts by executives who had no faith in either film, Lucas vowed to destroy the system from within so that he never again had to endure executives mutilating his film for non-filmic reasons. Like avant-garde artists whose goal was to explode the system in which they operated, Lucas's goal was to thwart the system and gain complete control over his films.

There were several qualities of *Star Wars* that made it an experimental film. First, Lucas insisted that the film have a documentary feel, meaning that it should look and feel as though shot on location. He employed multiple camera angles at once, allowing actors to drift into the scene as though the cameras were inadvertently picking up their presence. Lucas was very concerned with the audience feeling as though the universe in which *Star Wars* existed was a real universe. He wanted the film to have a newsreel quality and look old and used. The used universe quality that Lucas insisted upon became a trope of the genre, copied by nearly every science fiction film that came after. The oily, junk-filled world of *Star Wars*, along with its documentary-like quality, made the film look and feel totally different from anything that came before.

In order to achieve these same effects on a scale that could encompass large spaceships traveling in and out of the shot as an actor might, the special effects crew on *Star Wars* had to invent and build their electronics from scratch. In addition to the shots that necessitated new technologies, Lucas insisted that the sound of the film be literally new. He wanted every sound in the film to be an invented sound. He asked Ben Burtt to create a library of new sounds. Consequently, over the next three decades, Burtt created an entire database of sounds that influenced several generations of films and filmmaking.[44]

Even with the game-changing innovations he harnessed, Lucas felt the film was basically a very low-budget movie and only represented about 25 percent of his vision. Notwithstanding all the innovations, his contemporaries blamed him for an audience shift of appreciation from supposedly smaller, grittier, and more personal films to summer blockbusters. This charge was absurd, partly because *Star Wars was* small, gritty, and personal. As far as Lucas was concerned, it could not have been any smaller, grittier, or more personal. He could barely achieve what he wanted to with the budget that he had; he made it a point to make the film look gritty; and the genre of the film was something that he had wanted to do ever since he was a kid, reading comic books and watching *Flash Gordon* serials on television. This charge was leveled based on the elitist notion that science fiction was a subgenre, and popularity was a disqualifying factor for true art.

The initial reception to his film in the production phase clearly humbled Lucas. He preemptively rejected the idea that he was an artist: "My thing about art is that I don't like the word art because it means pretension and bullshit, and I equate those two directly . . . I don't think of myself as an artist, and I don't think I ever will . . . I'm a craftsman. I don't make a work of art; I make a movie. If it does what I want it to do then someone else can come along and figure it out."[45] It was after the first *Star Wars* film that Lucas began swearing that he had gotten all the big-budget films out of his system and that from then on he would leave the mainstream and only do personal, experimental films. These sorts of declarations point to a tension within Lucas regarding his dream of being a serious filmmaker—an auteur—as well as a successful one. His promises of smaller personal films became a sort of joke by the end of his career.

Lucas made distinctions between being a filmmaker and a film director, the idea being that he was more of a filmmaker than an auteur director. He even downplayed *Star Wars* itself and said that he only made the film to see whether he could. Clearly, the reception from his friends and contemporaries, as well as his wife, had gotten to him.[46] The irony of these announcements of being done with mainstream films was that Lucas soon completely left the mainstream studio system and made artsy, experimental films in other *Star Wars* films. The only reason no one thought they were artsy and experimental was because of the genre and their overwhelming popularity. Lucas may have tried to save face with his wife and friends by downplaying *Star Wars*, but he had made an original groundbreaking work of art.

In making *Star Wars*, Lucas stayed true to his nerd origins. For that reason, *Star Wars* was as much a small and personal film as *Taxi Driver* was for Scorsese. What Lucas had really wanted to do was get the rights to the *Flash Gordon* serials and make a feature film based on the space fantasy and science fiction that he loved as a kid. When King Features denied him the rights to *Flash Gordon*, *Star Wars* was born. Before *Star Wars* came out, Lucas bought a partnership in a comic books store in New York City called Supersnipe. Edward Summer, a graduate of New York University, co-owned and managed the store.[47]

Charles Lippincott, vice president of the *Star Wars* corporation's advertising, publicity, promotion, and merchandising, understood what sort of nerd Lucas was and, more importantly, what sort of nerd would be excited about his new film. Lippincott understood that Lucas clones were the obvious audience for *Star Wars*—kids and young adults who were into science fiction and comic books. In other words, nerds. It was Lippincott's idea to do a novelization of the film before the film's release. Lippincott also orchestrated a deal with Marvel comics that included a six-issue comic book adaptation of the film. Lippincott had to promise a skeptical Stan Lee that Marvel would not have to pay anything to Lucasfilm until the comics sold 100,000 copies. Lippincott used Ed Summer, co-owner of Supersnipe, as a go-between to get comics writer Roy Thomas on board. The novelization and the comic series both sold out before the film even appeared in theaters.[48] Lippincott was also the first film promoter to host a movie-related event at Comic-Con before the film was released. His promotion had a lot to do with *Star Wars* being a smash hit the day it opened.

The downside of embracing the types of fans who loved comic books and who frequented science fiction conventions was that *Star Wars* became low-hanging fruit for elitists in the industry who made their bones by ridiculing movies that they felt were low-culture popcorn films. *Star Wars* already had two strikes against it for being a space fantasy to begin with, and that coupled with its wide popularity ensured that some critics and other filmmakers would take a swipe at it, accusing it of not being a serious film, or worse, ruining the industry for other, more serious movies by monopolizing ticket sales. Even executives at Fox were initially leery of spending the kind of money that Lucas was asking for on a genre that they felt was out of style and costly in terms of the special effects certainly required.

Unsurprisingly, critics such as Vincent Canby of the *New York Times* found the film totally without depth, pandering to the lowest common denominator of filmgoer.[49] Science fiction writer Ben Bova opined that he was disappointed in Lucas's film, especially since Lucas had proven that he could make what Bova felt was a much more serious science fiction movie in *THX 1138*. Bova referred to *Star Wars* derisively as a Saturday morning shoot-em-up, which Lucas likely found to be right on point since its inspiration was the *Flash Gordon* serials. This was not the only time someone leveled a criticism at *Star Wars* that Lucas likely took as a compliment. *New Yorker* writer Pauline Kael once said that George Lucas was not in the moviemaking business at all but rather in the toy business. Criticisms like these were not piercing to a man who loved toys and whose father sold toys. Lucas at times likened *Star Wars* to an amusement park ride just like those he had created in his back yard as a kid, on which consumers wanted to ride several times.[50]

Lucas became agitated when critics tried to measure the film according to criteria in which he was clearly not interested. When the founder of the American science fiction magazine *Starlog*, Kerry O'Quinn, asked him whether he thought *Star Wars* was an important film and whether it changed peoples' lives, the question totally bewildered Lucas, and he bit back by saying that it was just a movie and that he hoped people enjoyed it like a sunset. He admonished critics and fans to stop analyzing it and just enjoy it.[51]

In the time of the American New Wave, film critics mattered, as did film criticism in general. Film criticism was part of the movement inspired by the French New Wave, whose flagship members Godard and Truffaut were themselves former film critics. Part of the saga of *Star Wars* centers on the transition from the importance of film critics such as Pauline Kael to fan-critics who dominated the internet and could profoundly affect the perception of a film. Lucas was never fond of critics such as Kael, but fan-critics ultimately destroyed him.

Creative writers in all genres are constantly told to write about what they know. In this way, stories become personal and authentic. Often authenticity is a guarantor of quality. In *Star Wars*, Lucas wrote about what he knew, what he had known ever since he was a kid. It just so happened that his personal authentic story was a space fantasy, and because of this, he had to struggle with the people closest to him thinking that he had sold out and muddied the waters for his contemporaries.

Lucas never really got the credit he deserved in the industry, especially from his peers. He certainly received financial credit from his fans, but critics and his fellow filmmakers never really acknowledged that Lucas had created a masterpiece, an unforgivable infraction by the snobby art elite. This eventually took its toll on the filmmaker, causing him to pull his movies ever closer and tighter to his chest.

Vincent Canby of the *New York Times* was one of the first critics to call *Star Wars* a popcorn flick—a term he may have coined—and charged Lucas, along with Spielberg, with dumbing down audiences and creating a taste for blockbuster films instead of important works of art. Joy Gould Boyum of the *Wall Street Journal* echoed Marcia Lucas's thoughts in saying that it was depressing that Lucas wasted his money and talent on such juvenile fare.[52] Peter Biskind's book *Easy Rider, Raging Bull* advanced the argument that Lucas and Spielberg broke away from other filmmakers like Scorsese and De Palma by making popcorn sci-fi flicks instead of gritty art films, and in doing so changed moviemaking forever.[53] Even Francis Ford Coppola asserted that *Star Wars* sidetracked Lucas from making films that were more experimental.[54]

What Lucas was trying to do by essentially leaving the studio system and creating movies on his terms was democratize the moviemaking process and place the power of filmmaking in the hands of the filmmakers, a Marxist program designed to reunite the worker with his or her product. An avant-garde artist is an elitist who is dedicated to an anti-elitist program with the ultimate goal of sharing the spoils of life.[55] An essential element of the avant-garde is an experimental spirit. Lucas was nothing if not experimental, especially with regard to technology.[56] An avant-garde artist, along with being experimental, is also revolutionary and is interested in revolutionizing the art form by exploding all formal traditions. He is like an enemy within a city, bent on destroying it.[57] The only reason that Lucas was not considered an avant-garde filmmaker was due to the notion that such a filmmaker rejects success and is not interested in creating masterpieces.

Despite some filmmakers and critics labeling *Star Wars* a blockbuster popcorn film and blaming the director for targeting the lowest common denominator of filmgoer, Lucas's 1977 film was a technologically avant-garde, experimental, and personal film created by an avant-garde and experimental filmmaker. That critics and filmmakers, many of whom claimed to be his friends, have cited

*Star Wars* as the culprit for dumbing down movies and shifting audience interest from grittier films to light, big-budget, summer blockbusters points to the low estimation of science fiction films and the villainization of the consumers and cultural base who love them. The story of *Star Wars* and its creator George Lucas has been informed by arbitrary designations of artistic production that assess some films and filmmakers as true artists, and others as low-brow fluff-makers and hacks. These unfair and inaccurate distinctions affected Lucas's personal and professional life, including his marriage, his relationships with his friends, his fandom, and especially his career and the *Star Wars* franchise. The success of *Star Wars* was a triumph of low culture and the attendant nerd culture that propped it up, as well as the triumph of a truly original artist whose experimental films just happened to be wildly popular, which disqualified them as avant-garde. The films also validated a fandom whose tastes had always been marginalized. The wild success of the film and the legions of nerds who adored it, coupled with the biting criticism that Lucas endured unexpectedly set the table for a conflict between the filmmaker and his fans, who before *Star Wars* was made were of a piece.

By the time *Star Wars* was released, Lucas had proven that his personal vision was not only authentic but that it also made money. Lucas and his buddy Spielberg managed to avoid the pitfalls of the era and stay true to themselves. The idea that Lucas and Spielberg ruined the American New Wave ignores the other baked-in viruses of the era, such as the rampant toxic masculinity and recklessness of many of the directors and star actors. Nevertheless, Lucas and Spielberg were not immune to the acculturation of the era. They were still very interested in being considered auteur filmmakers. Lucas would attempt to nurture this image in the coming years despite his public statements, even to the point of revising his films, to the dismay of his fans. He was still very insecure about his nerd persona and his manhood tied up in his auteur persona, so much so that when his fans began creating their own *Star Wars* stories replete with homosexual relationships between male characters, he went ballistic.

Lucas's buddy John Milius said that Lucas hated directing, that he was too sickly to direct, that he was always getting sick due to his diabetes. Milius said that Lucas always told him that he wished that he could just make porn, that porn was always shot in warm rooms, and if the location did not work, crews could simply move on to another warm room. According to Milius, had *Star Wars* not worked out, Lucas would own the porn industry. Porno, Lucas always said. That's the answer.[58]

# 3

# I HAVE A BAD FEELING ABOUT THIS

The origins of nerd fandom began with Hugo Gernsback, a man who came to New York in 1909 and founded the Wireless Association of America and *Modern Electronics*, the first known electronics and radio magazine.[1] Eventually, Gernsback began publishing short stories alongside articles concerning amateur wireless electronics. He called these stories "scientifiction" and, later, science fiction. Soon, the most prestigious award for science fiction writers was named the Hugo Award in honor of Gernsback. He would go on to publish many periodicals, but the one that really caught fire was *Amazing Stories*, first appearing in 1926. Along with publishing heavyweight science fiction writers like Jules Verne and H. G. Wells, Gernsback also included a very robust letters section of the magazine where fans could write in and discuss the stories in the magazine. These letter writers eventually led to clubs, which led to the conventions, which ushered in participatory fan and nerd culture.[2] By the 1930s, science fiction had grown as a popular literary and film genre, leading Forest J. Ackerman to coin the term "sci-fi." In 1939, the World Science Fiction Society created a large convention called Worldcon.

In the 1950s and 1960s, the Cold War and space race led to a plethora of films about monsters, mad scientists, and alien creatures, which attracted dedicated followings.[3] Alongside science fiction fandom emerged celebrity fandom, which focused more on individuals than cultural production. The two types of fandom wound up sharing many of the same stereotypes.

In the nineteenth century, the meaning of the term "celebrity" transformed from the condition of being famous to a famous individual. The development of photography in the mid-nineteenth century catalyzed this notion as celebrities such as Buffalo Bill made their way into the public's collective imagination. The invention of sound recording in 1878, cinema in 1889, and airwave broadcasting or radio in 1906 laid the foundation for celebrity fandom.[4] In 1910 *Motion Picture Story Magazine*, the first national movie magazine, was published and some of the first fan clubs emerged. Within five years, *Photoplay*, *Motion Picture*, and *Shadowland* also appeared. When Rudolph Valentino, one of the first major film stars, died in 1926, 75,000 people marched on his home after his funeral and trashed it, fueling the perception that fandom in general was dangerous.[5]

The term "fan" first appeared in late seventeenth-century England, where it was a common abbreviation for "fanatic" (a religious zealot). It became significant in the United States a century later when journalists used it to describe the passion of baseball spectators. This later usage was adopted to describe dedicated audiences for film and recorded music.[6] The word still carries with it the negative baggage of its original meaning.[7] Fandom, while necessary to the success of cultural production, has been viewed warily. Cultural producers love their fans—as long as they stay in their lane.

From the moment *Star Wars* came out, its fandom refused to stay in its lane. In many cases, because of negative stereotypes, fans have not been a trusted component in the entertainment equation. They have often been considered volatile and in need of control. Fans are supposed to be passive receptors of entertainment, not cultural agents with the power to affect the cultural artifacts that they love.

Fans have often been described as desexualized social outcasts. These are the same stereotypes associated with nerddom. The concept of a nerd as a type of person has existed in novels and plays going back hundreds of years, but the contemporary term did not make its first appearance until a *Newsweek* article in 1951 suggested that the word "nerd" was another slang term for a square.[8] The buzzword, along with its visual counterpart, did not hit the mainstream until a few decades later when *Saturday Night Live* first created its nerd sketch featuring Dan Aykroyd and then again six years later in the film *Revenge of the Nerds*. In the 1984 film the nerdy characters infiltrate a sorority and set up cameras in order to watch the girls sleep, something that now would be criminal. Nevertheless, it seems that there has always been a connection between technological ability and nerdiness. The film also highlights a relationship between nerdiness and sex. In the film, sexual desire is a prime motivation for the geeks because their nerdiness prevents them from fulfilling it. At the end of *Revenge of the Nerds*, not unlike what happens to Terry the Toad in *American Graffiti*, the quintessential nerd Louis has sex with the popular blonde cheerleader, demonstrating his sexual prowess and quipping at one point that jocks only think about sports while nerds only think about sex. *Revenge of the Nerds*, like *American Graffiti*, is a nerd fantasy.

Illustrative of this point is the hit show *The Big Bang Theory*, which presents a group of genius misfits, gifted in science and math, who love comic books. Some cite the popularity of this show as evidence that nerds and geeks are no longer the pariahs of the cultural order, but the show still presents STEM (science, technology, engineering, and math) abilities as odd, abnormal, weird, and freakish. Many scientists feel like the show is actually a step in the wrong direction and further stigmatizes STEM acumen and interest.[9] The marginalization of math and science—and folks with affinities for these disciplines—is a problem in American culture and is part of the reason why the United States tends to fall behind other countries in these areas.

A socially constructed dichotomy exists between sexual attractiveness and interest in science and technology. As their sexual organization develops, middle schoolers pick up the message that if one wants to have sex, then one should avoid science and math and strive for athletic success instead. Science and math, or nerddom in general, offers a safe haven from sexual expectations of any sort, functioning as a sort of closet.[10] Nerds are considered "sexually creepy" and unattractive, with no hope of ever getting a date.[11]

For most of his life, Lucas's relationship with sex has been shrouded in mystery. Even his wife Marcia suggested to one or more of George's friends that their marriage was sexless. John Baxter, in his biography of Lucas, related a story told by Richard Walter, a friend of Lucas's from his USC film school days, about chatting with Marcia once at a party. Walter conveyed that Marcia told him something that Walter had always suspected—that George was not interested in sex, and that Marcia found this very isolating. Walter said Marcia described her relationship with George as "Fortress Lucas" and said that she just could not stand the darkness any longer.[12]

There are essentially two types of nerds, the intellectual and the socially awkward. Lucas fit both definitions and only transcended his nerddom through his work, both with regard to his fantasies was well as his tremendous success that lifted him out of the ranks of the hopelessly nerdy. The work became the very thing that both identified him and inoculated him from nerddom. *Star Wars* offered street cred and a nerd badge as well as a pathway out of nerddom. Lucas eventually rejected nerddom and desperately tried to nurture his auteur image.

Since the dawn of the information age, the internet, and the dot-com boom, nerds began to transcend their lowly stature and flip the script with regard to what was cool. While the stereotypes and nerd/cool dichotomy suggests that smart people cannot be sexy, and sexy people cannot be smart, one could argue that culturally, this has changed with the popularity of *Star Wars*.

The explosion of *Star Wars* attracted all the strands of nerd fandom, including classic nerds drawn to STEM fields; the descendants of Gernsback, who were aficionados of science fiction and who frequented the comic-cons and led participatory fan culture; and celebrity worshippers.

Before long, repeated viewings and long lines became part of the experience of going to see *Star Wars*. Often audiences would just hang out for an hour and then watch the film again. This was not a typical thing for theaters to have to deal with. It was because of *Star Wars* that theaters began clearing the theaters in between showings.

From the first special effects shot, where the small ship Tantive IV attempts to outrun the massive Imperial Star Destroyer, fans cheered. In Champaign, Illinois, a physics doctoral student named Timothy Zahn was one of those fans who went bananas over the opening thirteen-second special effects shot. He would go on to be the most celebrated *Star Wars* writer of all time.[13] Zahn's *Thrawn Trilogy*, begun in 1991, helped bridge the gap between the original *Star Wars* trilogy and the prequels and introduced fans to the Expanded Universe and popular characters like General Thrawn and Mara Jade.

The manager of the Coronet Theater described *Star Wars* crowds in 1977 as "Old people, young people, children, Hare Krishna groups. They bring cards to play in line. We have checker players, we have chess players; people with paint and sequins on their faces. Fruit eaters like I've never seen before, people loaded on grass and LSD."[14] *Star Wars* just happened to coincide with the highest level of marijuana usage among high schoolers, which peaked in 1978 and has been dropping ever since.

Very soon, *Star Wars* replaced *Star Trek* as the hot science fiction film. The most obvious evidence of this was in the science fiction magazine *Starlog*, which devoted only one page to the film in June 1977 when the film debuted. After that, *Star Wars* dominated the pages, to the chagrin of some *Star Trek* fans. Many *Star Trek* fans almost immediately began publishing *Star Wars* fanzines after *Star Wars* debuted. The sense among the producers of these magazines, with names like *Moonbeam, Skywalker, Hyper Space,* and *Alderaan,* was that Lucasfilm was going to be much tougher in terms of copyright than *Star Trek* had been under the aegis of Paramount, which owned the *Star Trek* franchise. Craig Miller, who was the head of Lucasfilm's fan relations, made it clear early on that he was working on a policy about fanzines.

In the first six months after *Star Wars* played in theaters, Lucas received over 6,000 letters asking for everything from autographs and memorabilia to detailed histories of all the characters. Lucas realized that if he did not control the fan market, someone else would. Therefore, he created a fan club; for $5, a club member could receive four issues of a *Star Wars* newsletter, a poster, six 8 × 10 photos of the characters, a patch, and a pencil. Lucas stressed that, while some fans had devoted their lives to *Star Wars*, he had not. One day a fan entered Lucas's Los Angeles office with a knife, claiming that he cowrote *Star Wars* and demanding compensation. The deranged fan shouted that whoever did not believe him could take a look outside where he parked the Millennium Falcon.[15]

Lucas immediately put his stamp on his characters, making sure that they were licensed trademarks of Lucasfilm and that no one could legally wear *Star Wars* costumes and make a profit. Public appearances by characters were forbidden unless sanctioned by Lucasfilm, and characters were prohibited from selling anything but the movies.

Lucasfilm was blown away by the amount of fan fiction that arose almost immediately, stories written by fans that take place inside the *Star Wars* universe. Rather than being complacent, Lucasfilm set up a free licensing service to which fans could submit their fiction and receive feedback concerning the potential for copyright infringement. This was a colossal undertaking on the part of Lucasfilm and an indication of its concerns about licensing its product. The company employed several people whose job it was to review huge amounts of fan fiction. The communication between Lucasfilm and fanzines was cordial at first; the company requested copies of all fanzines to put in its archives. Lucasfilm even provided thank-you notes to the fanzines. The Lucasfilm licensing system in place since the 1970s offered fanzines licenses free of charge, reviewed the work, and offered criticism as well as considered copyright infringement.

This form of self-regulation was very similar to the Comics Code back in the 1950s, which was a self-regulating body created by the industry that required a stamp of approval on a comic in order to assure parents that a particular title was appropriate for kids. Fanzines began to police themselves like the comics in the 1950s did. For comics, the code had devastating effects that still reverberate to this day. The code forced artists and writers to avoid complicated adult storylines for fear of not being sanctioned by the Comics Code. As a result, comics churned out formulaic storylines and one-dimensional characters that failed to garner much interest among adults.

Meanwhile, *Star Wars* was blowing up coast to coast. In New York, mounted police were called in to control the crowds. Johnny Cash, Muhammad Ali, and Ted Kennedy all waited in line. Right before he died, Elvis was in the process of trying to get a print of the film for himself to view at Graceland. Apparently, the King found it too inconvenient to wait in line at the theater like everyone else.

Elvis died without ever seeing the film. Soon there appeared to be a wave effect regarding the success of the film. Word of mouth brought in the die-hard science fiction fans, and then anecdotal stories about long lines and celebrity sightings brought in everyone else. Soon a cultural phenomenon was taking place.

Once it was clear that *Star Wars* was a hit, Lucas set out to create his own ranch for his new independent film company. He found a piece of property about fifty-five miles south of San Francisco called Bulltail Ranch on Lucas Valley Road, named after John Lucas, a settler who had received the land as a wedding gift in 1882. As Lucas walked the property in 1978, he told his accountants that he wanted to buy it. This was where he would build Skywalker Ranch.

Not long after the film opened, Harrison Ford arrived at director Jeremy Kagan's house with his shirt nearly torn off. When asked what happened, Ford, a little shaken up, said he had simply gone into Tower Records to pick up an album, and adoring fans attacked him.[16] It was the Hollywood version of the British invasion. Everyone associated with the film became celebrities. Even the special effects guys at Lucasfilm's visual effects subsidiary, Industrial Light and Magic, were hit up for autographs. The stars of the film, like Ford, did not dare venture outside for fear of mobbing fans. Todd Hansen described the film as "twenty times cooler than whatever the last coolest thing we'd ever seen had been. . . . It dwarfed whatever it was it had put into second place—you couldn't even *see* second place. Second place was somewhere off the bottom of the page."[17]

Before long, even the soundtrack was certified gold.[18] Almost immediately, fans were wondering about a sequel. Lucas said, "At first I was contemplating selling the whole thing to Fox to do whatever they wanted with it . . . I'd just take my percentage and go home and never think about *Star Wars* again. But the truth of it is I got captivated by the thing. It's in me now."[19] The United States had not seen this sort of craze since the Beatles. By Labor Day 1977, *Star Wars* had sold over $133 million in ticket sales from under 1,000 theaters. Darth Vader, Threepio, and Artoo had their names and footprints set in concrete at Mann's Chinese Theatre.

*Star Wars* added $20 million to Lucas's net worth, and, along with the merchandising income, Lucasfilm became a $30 million corporation. Lucas bought a Ferrari and allotted himself $50,000 a year to live on.[20] While the $50,000 seemed rather conservative, the Ferrari pointed to a masculinity in need of a boost. Another surprising phenomenon was that audiences loved Darth Vader.

Lucas realized that Vader was a strong villain, but he had no idea the character would be so popular. Even Lucas admitted that Darth Vader had taken over. Because of Vader's immense popularity, it became clear that he would have to play a much larger role in the subsequent films and that Lucas would need to expand on his mythology. In the first film, he was a mere tool of the dark side. In the sequels, he would rule the galaxy. Vader took over a story that was supposed to be about Luke, a version of its creator. Instead, the story became about Vader, another version of its creator as well as an omen of things to come.

A growing and lively underground fan base of science fiction culture felt as though Lucas made the movie specifically for them. Jon Davidson, the producer of the *Robocop* films, noted that Lucas drew on a whole generation of kids from across the country who were in their twenties and wanted to do special effects. These were kids who worked in their garages and loved effects and fantasy movies. Many had done a commercial here or there, or nothing professional at all. They were waiting for someone like Lucas to show them the way. They were a motivated and eager workforce and would have worked on something like *Star Wars* for nothing. In 1973 and 1974, the Academy did not even hand out an award for special effects. The studios were not bothering with the costly production required. When the studios did incorporate effects, they were not very good.[21]

Many kids spent the months after seeing the film writing their own stories, playing with action figures, and dressing up in costumes. The experience was so profound that it eventually influenced career paths for many young people.[22] Soon after the first film was released, there began a sort of competition to see who was the bigger fan, measured by who could quote more of the film.

Lucasfilm and the company's *Star Wars* marketing director, Charles Lippincott, seduced young fans in ways that are still resonating today. Before the release of the film, Lippincott approached several toy companies and tried to sell them on the idea of action figures. At the time, there were a few companies that sold action figures, such as Mego Corporation, which produced Action Jackson and the World's Greatest Superheroes. By late February 1977, Lippincott was not getting much interest in a toy line connected to the upcoming film and was even asked to leave a Mego booth at a toy fair because of his persistence. Finally, Lippincott received some interest from Kenner, a Cincinnati-based company that had invented the Easy Bake Oven and a twelve-inch action figure called the Six Million Dollar Man based on the television show with the same name starring Lee Majors. Kenner made the *Star Wars* deal mostly out of the hope that *Star Wars* would be made into a television show like *Six Million Dollar Man*. The CEO of Kenner, Bernie Loomis, and Lippincott signed a deal one month before the release of the film, promising that Kenner would produce four action figures as well as a family game. The exact parameters of the deal were shaky, and sometimes referred to as "fifty bucks and a handshake."[23] Lucas was upset that

Lucasfilm was not able to keep more of the money, but Lippincott impressed upon him that no one wanted to make a deal at all.

At the time, a line of 3.75-inch-tall action figures called Micronauts was selling well, so Kenner decided to make *Star Wars* action figures the same size. The figures needed to be able to fit into spaceships, and if the figures were a foot high, then the spaceships would have to be four times that size. Once it was clear that the movie was a smash hit, Kenner scrambled to release the action figures in time for the holiday season. They would have to start shipping the figures in August in order to be on the shelves in time for Christmas shoppers. Kenner quickly realized that this was going to be an impossibility. A junior-level executive came up with the plan to have an "early bird special," a $10 piece of cardboard promising four action figures just as soon as Kenner made them. Lucas quickly signed an additional deal with Kenner for more toys, including the all-important blasters, despite Loomis having banned guns from the Kenner line following the Vietnam War.

In 1978, Kenner sold more than forty-two million *Star Wars* items, twenty-six million of which were the action figures. By 1985, there were more *Star Wars* figures than U.S. citizens.[24] Image Factory also struck early by offering Lucas $100,000 up front for the exclusive rights to market posters, buttons, and iron-on decals. Prior to their foray into the merchandising business, the company had primarily dealt in rock band T-shirts. By the end of 1978, a poster of Darth Vader wielding his lightsaber outsold Image Factory's former leading poster, featuring Farrah Fawcett in a red swimsuit. Darth Vader, a man more machine than human, was more popular than the pinup girl Farrah Fawcett. The company made over $600,000 on the *Star Wars* deal.[25] Lucas had infiltrated a culture on a deep and fundamental level.

From the very beginning, Lucas envisioned merchandise from the film. He thought *Star Wars* would be similar to what he called the "Davy Crockett phenomenon," where kids became enamored with the 1950s television show following the exploits of the frontiersman and pined for the coonskin hat for sale. Lucas struck deals with Coca-Cola, Burger Chef, and other companies to release lunchboxes, trading cards, and dishware, but he made it clear that he was not interested in slapping the *Star Wars* logo on just anything. He set up a subsidiary called Black Falcon to oversee all merchandising. He did not want the market glutted with junk bearing the *Star Wars* name. The merchandise had to meet a certain Lucasfilm standard. For example, Lucas turned down cheap jewelry and toilet seat covers, surprising Fox, which felt that any deal that involved revenue was a good deal.

As Kenner scrambled to meet the demand for the Early Bird certificates for Christmas 1977, its market research department conducted a survey of 1,000 children. The toymaker's staggering findings suggested that one-third of the kids had already seen the movie, and nearly half of those had seen it more than once. The kids who had not seen the film were desperate to see it. Almost immediately, a new cultural lingua franca dominated the social circuit. When a child spent the night with a friend, they invariably played *Star Wars*, and when the action figures came out, they played with them. Kids brought *Star Wars* toys to school and kept them in their desks. When it rained and kids could not play outside, they played with the *Star Wars* toys inside the classroom. Kids who had not seen the film were left behind and out of touch with this new magical world.

As millions upon millions of action figures flooded the market, *Star Wars* as a mythology was making an indelible mark on the minds of a whole generation of kids. Within the first two years, in addition to the action figures, Kenner released the spaceships, including the X-wing, TIE-fighter, and the Millennium Falcon. The action figures and ships played a major role in continuing the narrative of the films after fans left the theaters. The movies continued outside the canonical films when the children played with the toys. New stories unfolded as kids directed the action figures and spaceships through narratives of their own. In this way, fans of the film began to feel a sense of ownership vis-à-vis the films, unlike anything that had come before.

Within a capitalist economy, creatives are in a constant power struggle with the capitalists who own the means of production. While the creators of a product tyrannically reign supreme regarding their authorship, the owners of the production reign supreme in terms of distribution of that product. Fans are left out of the equation. The popularity of the toys accelerated the eventual conflict between Lucas and his fans because the toys implanted a creator sense within the psyche of the fans. The toys awoke in fans a taste for playing the role of creator and thereby engendered a sense of ownership that ran afoul of the model by which Lucas and the studio retained the sole rights to the creative experience.

Meaning can only happen once a consumer engages with a cultural artifact. The moviegoer may be thought of as a cocreator of a film. This is the case regardless of the quality of the film. The act of playing with the action figures represented a continuation of the movie theater experience. The action figures, while still replete with Lucas's intentions insofar as they still carried the vestiges of his intended characterizations, became untethered from the narrative of the films as kids played with them. The viewer became author as well as viewer as he or she engaged with the toys in an endless recursive narrative.

Lucas's original role was lessened as whoever controlled the action figures was free to alter the narrative at will.

The narrative possibilities of the toys were limitless. For many kids, *Star Wars* action figures dominated their play. Sometimes kids mixed them with other action figures from other film franchises, like *GI Joe* or *The Lone Ranger*. For the most part, fans maintained Lucas's characterization. For example, Han Solo was typically never the villain. Vader always was. The settings were crucial, as fans played with the action figures outside in the snow or in the dirt. Some children set up block forts and orchestrated wars wherein they would employ rubber bands as the primary weapon and go from side to side shooting down each figure until all the figures on one side were toppled and a winner emerged. Kids slept with the action figures. Some would set them up in the bathtub and run the water; the one that stayed on his or her feet the longest was the victor.

In 1979 sales of the toys, including the action figures, spaceships, and play-sets brought in more than $200 million, injecting more than $20 million into the Lucasfilm subsidiary Black Falcon. The income from the toys ensured that Lucas would make the sequel.[26] In fact, without the money from the merchandise, there is a good chance the sequel would not have been made at all, or at least would not have been made as soon as it was or as well. Lucas invested everything that he had into the second film.

According to film producer Gary Kurtz, plans for the sequel were not solidified until it was clear a month into the *Star Wars* release that it was going to be a hit. At that point, Lucas decided that he had a franchise on his hands.

For his next film, he would leave the studio system completely and finance the film himself. The only thing 20th Century Fox would be responsible for was distribution, just as Dennis Hopper did with *Easy Rider*. This was a true game-changer, and another example of how Lucas was more of a rogue filmmaker than the very folks who claimed that he ruined movies for rogue filmmakers. Lucas forced Fox into giving him the final cut on the second film as well as all the merchandising rights. Eventually, Fox's share was less than 25 percent. Lucas noted excitedly that when the shoe was on the other foot, the studios felt completely betrayed.[27]

The first draft of *The Empire Strikes Back* was an outlined nine-page treatment. Much of the structure for the film was in this very first treatment. Lucas had several scenes in mind that would survive all the way through to the final draft. There would be a gambler from Han's past who would invite Han, Leia, and Chewie to dinner—unbeknownst to them, as guests of Vader. Luke would study the force under the tutelage of an old Jedi master. Luke would also battle Vader and wind up hanging from the bottom of a city in the sky. In the treatment, Three-pio is destroyed and Luke has a twin sister, but it is not clear that she is Leia.

After the torture of writing *Star Wars*, Lucas was determined to turn the task of writing the screenplay over to someone else. In late November 1977 he called in Leigh Brackett, a science fiction novelist who wrote the screenplays for *The Big Sleep*, *Hatari!*, and *Rio Lobo*, all films Lucas admired. For several days in late November and early December, Lucas and Brackett discussed Lucas's treatment and brainstormed additional plot details. On December 2, Brackett—who was paid a flat fee of $50,000—took Lucas's notes and went off to write the first draft. Brackett delivered the first draft of *The Empire Strikes Back* on February 21. Lucas was disappointed. While Brackett had largely followed his treatment, he felt it was wrong. Three weeks later, Brackett died of cancer. Lucas and Marcia took a trip to Mexico where Lucas rewrote the script. In three weeks he had a new version and sent it over to Alan Ladd at 20th Century Fox. In this version, Vader reveals his paternity to Luke. Boba Fett also appears in this version of the script. Lucas based the bounty hunter on Clint Eastwood's Man with No Name character from the Sergio Leone westerns. Part of the reason for creating Boba Fett was that Kenner begged for a character that they could release before the film. Boba Fett, with his cool costume and assortment of gear, was an ideal action figure. The toyetic vision of the character brought Fett to life. The character was specifically created for employment by fans in their own constructed narratives, irrespective of the canonical films. Boba Fett never had much dialogue in the films; his character life mostly took place outside of the canonical films.

Brackett's death left Lucas in a lurch as far as having a screenwriter who could put the finishing touches on the script. As a result, Lucas called on Lawrence Kasdan, who had just written the screenplay for *Raiders of the Lost Ark* for Lucas and Spielberg. Lucas hired him to finish up *Empire* before even reading Kasdan's script for *Raiders*. By midsummer, Kasdan completed about twenty-five pages of the screenplay. Kasdan, Lucas, and Gary Kurtz began poring over the manuscript and figuring out which ideas were worth pursuing.

With the unexpected fame and popularity of Darth Vader, whose role in the first film was as a mere henchman, it became clear that Darth's role in the second film needed to expand. Lucas admitted that directing took too much out of him and that he was completely exhausted. As a result, he decided to turn over the directorial reigns to someone else. Lucas abandoned the very thing that meant so much to him as a filmmaker at USC—the notion of the auteur as director. He no longer seemed to care. He would finance the film and generally supervise but leave all the grunt work to his minions. Because of the wild success of *American Graffiti* and *Star Wars*,

Lucas no longer seemed to care about auteurism. Everyone knew who was responsible for *Star Wars*. He had made his bones. He was now unassailable. He had solidified himself as a successful filmmaker beyond anyone's wildest dreams, even his own. What compelled him to want to be considered an auteur in the first place—respect, admiration, and love—were all sated. He achieved what he wanted to and now could bask in the spoils without driving his frail body to the brink of collapse. He could afford to relinquish the directing duties to someone else without giving up his creator reputation.

Perhaps the biggest cinematic moment in the *Star Wars* saga occurs toward the end of *The Empire Strikes Back* when Darth Vader reveals that he is Luke's father. Lucas created this plot point while writing *Empire*, setting in motion the prequels and the transformation of Darth Vader, a transformation that only retrospectively became the most important character arc of the film, nudging out Luke Skywalker, whose character arc would later be completely botched in *Episode VIII* under the aegis of Disney and then completed with *Episode IX*. Lucas was concerned that the shocking revelation would traumatize his younger fans. He consulted psychologists, who told him that those who could not deal with it would think Vader was lying.[28] Vader's shifting importance in the film, as well as Lucas's deep concern about the audience reaction, suggests that Lucas was still very much in tune with how audiences might feel and was willing to adjust the narrative accordingly. In this way, fans have always had a say in the narratives of the films.

The plot point concerning Vader as Luke's father was key in launching the *Star Wars* franchise beyond the first trilogy, as it pointed to a past that was crucial to the events of the present. Lucas was interested in establishing *Star Wars* as a mythology born whole from the mind of a genius. In order to perpetuate the idea that he had conceived of the project beforehand, Lucas immediately changed the title of *The Empire Strikes Back* from *Episode II* to *Episode V* in order to suggest that the prequels were always part of the plan. At this point, Lucas subtitled the original *Star Wars* film, *A New Hope*.

In November 1979, the very first published script of the first movie was released with a publication date of 1976 and the title *Episode IV: A New Hope*, suggesting that Lucas had conceived of this title as far back as 1976, when in reality the title was not created until 1979. Lucas already began altering the original film, something for which fans eventually vilified him, especially when these changes started to affect the film and story itself. The published script was not the revised fourth script of the film at all but rather a sort of transcribed shooting script of the actual film. The result of these little changes was an alternative history of the *Star Wars* franchise, one in which Lucas conceived a complete *Star*

*Wars* universe, including its major characters and their histories. Lucas in effect retconned[29] *Star Wars* with *The Empire Strikes Back*, and then denied that he had done so. He would comment around the time of *Empire* that the story arc could be described as the tragedy of Darth Vader, when in actuality the story initially was called *The Adventures of Luke Skywalker*.

Lucas was interested in establishing a myth of the franchise and drawing a line in the sand in regard to creative control and authority. The story was his and his alone, and any changes that he made were fake news and were there all along. Lucas effectively engaged in a sort of Orwellian control of his films with the goal of asserting his own authority and genius. The choice to increase Vader's role in the films was due to audiences loving the character. Arguably, the *Star Wars* franchise and the direction in which it went regarding Vader's story arc was a result of fan influence rather than Lucas's vision. Part of mythmaking involves hiding the constructed origins. Lucas clearly embraced this idea of a myth as religion. Masking the origins of his story and purporting that it came to him as twelve whole stories, not unlike the murky origins of religions, relies on an incredibly arrogant self-appointed prophet or God.

Lucas was interested in infusing the second film with overt religious symbolism, such as when Vader lures Luke to the dark side in a dream. Luke beheads his own father and finds his own face in the mask, anticipating his own temptation to the dark side and evoking the devil's temptation of Christ in the desert.

Director Irvin Kershner began filming *Episode IV* in Finse, Norway, in March 1979. Fierce blizzards, even for Norway, battered the production. While Lucas insisted he was done directing, he hovered over Kershner during principal shooting. He also oversaw the editing process. The amount of scrutiny and fan support of the film deeply affected Lucas; he noted to Lawrence Kasdan, "Every little sentence has been gone over and speculated upon and looked at sixteen different ways."[30] Auteur director or not, this was Lucas's baby.

In June 1979, Lucas traveled to England to see a rough cut of *Empire*. He did not like what he saw. He felt that Kershner was trying to make too good of a movie and that it was a lot better than he wanted it to be. Lucas cut half of the footage from the first eighty minutes, and when he showed his version to Kershner, Paul Hirsch, and Gary Kurtz, they criticized it mercilessly. Lucas exploded and yelled, "You guys are ruining my picture! . . . It's my money, it's my film, and I'm going to do it the way I want to do it!"[31] These guys were the director, editor, and producer whom Lucas had hired to create the film. This was not a good day or a good look for Lucas, who seemed like the little, spoiled, sawed-off brat who lost his temper when his buddies broke his roller coaster in his back yard. He referred to himself as the super-editor and worried that even he could not save the film—a film that wound up being the best one of the bunch by a long shot, according to nearly everyone. By the time the movie was made, it cost Lucas over $33 million of his own money and was the costliest film ever made by an independent filmmaker. Despite Lucas's annoyances, Kershner completed principal photography on September 24, 1979.

Lucas and his team again had to invent the technology to achieve his vision for the film. To this end, he created an entire computer graphics division of Lucasfilm. The division focused on creating the digital tools to make the film. By 1985, the group headed by Ed Catmull created a Pixar image computer with which they could make animated movies. After the first run of his trilogy, Lucas was a little cash-strapped and wound up selling the Pixar image computer as well as his entire graphics computer division, including Catmull, to Steve Jobs. Catmull pointed out before taking the job with Lucas that he and his staff were huge fans of *Star Wars* and considered it a dream to work for the visionary avant-garde filmmaker, noting that Lucas was the only filmmaker in or out of Hollywood who invested seriously in film technology.[32] Steve Jobs bought the Pixar computer and the graphics division for $35 million and turned it into a multibillion dollar company that produced a parade of hit animated films, including the immensely popular *Cars* and *Toy Story* franchises.

*The Empire Strikes Back* opened on Wednesday, May 21, 1980, in 126 theaters. Even though Fox quietly expected *Empire* to do about a third of the business of the first *Star Wars*, the film premiered at Grauman's Egyptian Theatre on Hollywood Boulevard not far from the Chinese Theatre and ran continuously for the first twenty-four hours. *Star Wars* fan club members began lining up three days ahead of time, and the film broke first-day records in 125 theaters across the United States. This time critics loved the film. Even the caustic Pauline Kael noted,

> There is no sense that this ebullient, youthful saga is running thin in imagination or that it has begun to depend excessively on its marvelous special effects—that it is in any danger, in short, of stiffening into mannerism or mere billion dollar style. I'm not sure if I'm up to seven more *Star Wars* adventures (I'm pretty sure my son is) but I can hardly wait for the next one.[33]

*Star Wars* received cover notoriety from *Time* magazine, but in a portending move, the face on the cover was not that of George Lucas or Luke Skywalker, but rather Darth Vader.[34] This move symbolized not only the transitional focus of the story from Luke to Vader but also the governing symbol of Lucas himself as his career followed the path of Vader.

While working on *The Empire Strikes Back*, Lucas began accumulating his own empire, hiring employees and purchasing facilities. He eventually bought a building on Lankershim Boulevard in Los Angeles. The building housed a former egg company, and so Lucas began calling it the Egg Company. Lucas was officially a part of Hollywood, something that he vowed never to be. He noted, "Everything has mushroomed. . . . Before, I had these modest dreams. Now I'm sitting on top of a corporation that is taking up a lot of my time. I've had to hire people and start new hierarchies, new bureaucracies, new everything to make the whole thing work." He also noted, "I had to become self-sufficient . . . I had to build an empire simply to make the movies the way I wanted to make them."[35]

Within three months of the film's release, Lucas made his money back. From the point of view of the average moviegoing kid, the film was awesome. Lucas had literally bet the ranch on the sequel and won.

The film closed out 1980 as the year's biggest film, grossing over $200 million in its first run, which made it the third most successful movie of all time, trailing only the original *Star Wars* and *Jaws*. Many to this day believe that *Empire* is the best of all the *Star Wars* movies, a film that essentially celebrates the failures of its protagonists.

*The Empire Strikes Back* initiates the focal transition from the nerd Luke to the all-powerful Darth Vader. The transition also reflects the life of George Lucas, as he began to view himself more as a titan and lord of an empire rather than a nerdy farm boy with his eye on the horizon. Even in the initial crawl, Vader is given top billing, as it is his desire to find Luke Skywalker and root out the rebellion that provides the narrative thrust of the film. Once again, Luke proves a weak hero, as he immediately requires rescue by Han Solo, who has usurped Luke's role as the princess's love interest.

In addition to representing Lucas's newfound power as overlord of his now Death Star–like franchise, *The Empire Strikes Back* also offers clues and insights into Lucas's personal life. For example, the Exogorth or space slug that the Millennium Falcon flies into with Han, Leia, Chewie, Threepio, and Artoo represents a deep and threatening *vagina dentata* that threatens to swallow the heroes whole. The heroes are on the run throughout the film as Vader relentlessly hunts them down, ultimately literally freezing in carbonite any potential for romance. The film ends as a neutered Luke looks into space along with Leia, whom unbeknownst to him, is really his sister.

With the success of *The Empire Strikes Back*, Lucas was all in on the *Star Wars* franchise, and it was not long before he began to think about a third film in what would become the original trilogy. One week before *The Empire Strikes*

*Back* premiered, Lucas announced that he already had a title for the third film, *Revenge of the Jedi*—which would eventually change to *Return of the Jedi* since, according to Lucas, Jedis do not seek revenge. Lawrence Kasdan would once again write the screenplay. Lucas had no clue about what would happen in the film. Harrison Ford urged Lucas to kill his character off, saying "He's got no mama, no papa, and he's got no story. . . . Let's kill him and get some weight to this thing,"[36] but Lucas would not acquiesce, fearing that if he did, he would alienate the many fans of the irresistible rogue. He did not want kids playing with the action figure of a dead character. Many lamented that George made dramatic film decisions based on toyetic variables.[37] Both the characters of Boba Fett and Han Solo were driven more by concerns about the toys than the story.

Once Gary Kurtz realized that George intended to make another attack on the Death Star a major plot point in the film, he was out as producer. He felt it was redundant. Lucas attempted to tap David Lynch to direct *Return of the Jedi*. Lynch was a filmmaker whose career represented an alternative to Lucas's; his own career nearly stalled after making excellent and unique films like *Eraserhead* and *The Elephant Man*. He was then given the enormous project of directing *Dune*, a film that wound up totally incoherent and bloated due to the studios mucking it up. Right before taking the *Dune* project, Lucas offered Lynch *Jedi*. What ensued was hilarious. Lynch visited Lucas at Skywalker Ranch, took a ride in his Ferrari, and then had lunch at a local salad bar. By the time the meeting was over, Lynch suffered a migraine and panic attack. He crawled into a phone booth and called his agent, howling that there was absolutely no way he could do the film. He realized that George's world was George's world and that there was no room in that world for anyone else. Lucas was far from the man who had made the Lynchian film *THX 1138*. David Lynch would go on to be one of the most uncompromising and excellent film directors in American film history, creating the sort of small personal films that Lucas always said he wanted to make.[38]

Rather than a visionary director such as Lynch, Lucas decided to tap a workhorse and someone who would not mind a little direction himself. Lucas wanted a television guy, as it was common in television for the director to be subservient to the executive producer. As far as Lucas was concerned, the age of the auteur director was a thing of the past when it came to who would be directing *Star Wars* films.

In early 1981, Lucas watched the thriller *Eye of the Needle* by the Welsh director Richard Marquand, who had spent much of his career directing television movies, including the 1979 biopic, *Birth of the Beatles*. Like Lynch, Marquand was also invited to the ranch, and spent the entire day with Lucas, eating dinner and talking late into the evening. Lucas thought Richard was a director he would feel comfortable with, one who would understand that it was really George's movie. Lucas also liked that Marquand was respected and well regarded for bringing projects in on time and on budget. Mostly Lucas felt like Marquand would be willing to toe the line in relation to Lucas's vision for the movie.

For the third film, Lucas wanted to write the entire script himself first, rather than just hand off a story treatment to a screenwriter. However, writing was still extremely difficult for him, and he left much of the details to his preferred screenwriter, Lawrence Kasdan. Lucas was not entirely sure that Kasdan would take the job, since his recent film *Body Heat* was successful, and he was now a proven Hollywood commodity. Lucas need not have worried, as Kasdan immediately accepted the work.

In early summer 1981, Lucas invited Kasdan and Marquand out for a story meeting. There were several elements Lucas knew he needed. He wanted to feature Jabba the Hutt since he finally had the resources to create the character he had envisioned for the first film. He wanted Luke to have a twin sister, though he still was not certain it was Leia. He also wanted a Wookie-like society helping the rebels.

For a time Lucas bought into screenwriter Lawrence Kasdan's advice that a major character in *Return of the Jedi* needed to die. That character was to be Lando Calrissian. The crew worried about how they were going to tell Billy D. Williams, similar to their apprehension in letting Alec Guinness know that Obi-Wan Kenobi would die in the first *Star Wars*. Eventually Lucas decided to have Yoda die of old age and spare Lando.

As Kasdan was hammering out the rest of the script, Lucas and his legal team worked on the legal and financial negotiations with 20th Century Fox, which had been dragging on for nearly two years. With Alan Ladd now out of the picture, Lucas took a hard line, and discussions were heated. Fox complained that the percentage of the profits Lucas was offering was so low that the studio would not have much incentive to promote the film. Lucas had little sympathy for Fox's complaints and little patience since, once again, he was going to be putting all of his own money in the film. After tying up nearly all his *Empire* profits in the ranch, Lucas did not have enough on hand to cover the $30 million he thought it would take to make the third film. This gave Fox leverage, but Lucas was not going to make it easy on the studio. When negotiations between Lucasfilm and Fox began to collapse, Lucas gave Fox an ultimatum. He gave the studio thirty days to make a decision after which, if no decision was made, he would take his movie to another studio.

Once Lucas arrived in London, he all but took over the film from Richard Marquand. The sense on the set was that Richard was not getting it, so Lucas never left. Lucas intimidated Marquand, who said that it was like directing King Lear with Shakespeare in the next room.[39] Lucas knew that he was getting in Marquand's way, but he did not care. From his point of view, Marquand was essentially making a film that had already been made. Lucas knew he would have final say in any scenario. The cast and crew came to Lucas for direction and guidance instead of the actual director. In this sense, Lucas was the auteur, though not in name. Lucas could finally have his cake and eat it, too.

Marquand was reduced to standing around. He tried to put on his best face and insist that he appreciated Lucas's input. Most mornings, Lucas asked to see Marquand's shot list for the day, something most directors closely guard. Lucas insisted that Marquand film in the documentary style Lucas used on *A New Hope*, with multiple cameras catching the action from various angles, so that Lucas would have plenty of shots to choose from in post-production.

The final weeks were spent on location in the desert around Yuma, Arizona, and the redwoods of Crescent City, California. To keep the production a secret, Lucas and Lucasfilm's marketing department had hats, clipboards, and film cans labeled with the name of a horror movie called *Blue Harvest*. The façade quickly fell away in Yuma when dune buggy enthusiasts caught a glimpse of Harrison Ford on Jabba the Hutt's enormous skiff.

Lucas was particularly frustrated with the mouth of the Sarlacc, visible at the bottom of an enormous pit dug into the desert sand. Lucas debated whether the monster should be visible at all and complained about the cost. The final creature—a large mouth lined with rows of teeth—was horrifying, and it bore enough of a resemblance to a certain body part that Carrie Fisher took to referring to it as the sand vagina, to Lucas's chagrin. Lucas was at the end of his rope. He was not having any fun and complained that he was the only person who seemed to know anything about *Star Wars*. He could not understand why he had to answer an endless amount of questions daily, despite telling everyone exactly what he wanted. He frustratingly announced that he was in too deep to stop. He vowed that the next trilogy would be made by someone else. He was done. By being present on the set, Lucas made himself available for questions. To ignore the fountainhead of the film franchise would have been disrespectful. He made himself indispensable.

Principal photography on *Return of the Jedi* wrapped in mid-May 1982. As advertised, Marquand brought the film in on time and on budget. It soon became clear that part of what was bothering Lucas was that his marriage was falling apart. Lucas told *Rolling Stone* that he was aware that the schedule was very hard on Marcia, and that the emotional stress that he was under was not helping things.[40] Longtime Lucas marketing director Charles Lippincott noted that Marcia had confided that George could not leave the stresses of filmmaking in the editing room, and that he brought those stresses to bed with him. She likened George's films to another woman who was getting all George's time and energy, with nothing left over for Marcia.[41]

In the late summer of 1982, the couple gave up on trying to have a child of their own and decided to adopt. Marcia eventually left Lucas in 1983 for an artist named Tom Rodriguez, whom Lucas hired to create the stained glass windows in his library on Skywalker Ranch. He was nine years younger than Marcia and evidently, in Marcia's eyes, a real artist. The impact of Marcia leaving Lucas was devastating, and was worsened by the fact that she left him for an artist who apparently had not sold out and who was interested in sex. Lucas's marriage was falling apart. Nevertheless, with *Return of the Jedi* Lucas had entered whole hog into the world of merchandising, as more than fifty licenses were handed out for everything from cream rinse to vases.

In *Return of the Jedi*, Vader makes his primacy known by being the first major character to appear on the screen. Luke's development into a Jedi is pronounced, but only in order to facilitate Vader's ultimate redemption at the end of the film, when he saves Luke by throwing the all-powerful emperor down an airshaft, killing him. Fans bemoaned the fate of Darth Vader, whose mass killings and destruction seemed to be completely forgiven. Similar to the Exogorth in *The Empire Strikes Back*, in *Return of the Jedi* the heroes are threatened by the massive gaping mouth of the Sarlacc, the tentacles of which look like pubic hairs wiggling from a diseased vagina, as Fisher had noted. A quick glimpse of the Sarlacc as it emerges from the maw reminds one of a protruding clitoris. Notably, the character Boba Fett meets his unlikely demise in the Sarlacc pit. By the end of film production, Lucas was deeply depressed about his failed marriage and, when asked about Boba Fett, told his director to just to throw him in the pit.

Obi-Wan's point that he told Luke the truth about his father from a certain point of view represents Lucas's narrative backpedaling in relation to the trilogy's story arc. Threepio's regaling of the adventures of Luke Skywalker and the rest of the rebels to the Ewoks is an exercise in the very legend-making that Lucas was always interested in creating. In this manner, *Return of the Jedi* reflects its creator, George Lucas, in its overt symbolism of the perils of love, his interest and insecurities in regard to myth-making, and his ultimate self-redemption, as Darth Vader comes full circle from a Jedi to a Sith and back to a Jedi. Just as fans were not immediately forgiving of Darth Vader for his murderous transgressions, they were equally suspicious of Lucas, who would soon betray them and alter the deal irrevocably.

The opening of *Return of the Jedi* on Wednesday, May 25, 1983, was officially an event. The cliffhangers from *Empire* had audiences lining up days in advance, counting down the hours, minutes, and seconds until the film premiered, and they could see how everything turned out. Lucas was finished with the trilogy. He had gained a lot and lost a lot.

As expected, *Return of the Jedi* was a smash hit. It made $6 million on its opening day in over 1,000 theaters. There were reports that fans camped out at theaters overnight to be the first in line, something that was unheard of at the time. By the end of the opening week, the film made $45 million and by the end of the year, $250 million. On top of that, the *Star Wars* Fan Club hit 184,000 members, and the novelization of the film was the best-selling book in the United States.

An admirer of Joseph Campbell and especially his book *A Hero with a Thousand Faces*, which Lucas read just after *A New Hope* to help him map out the quest of his characters, Lucas met and screened the trilogy for Campbell. After watching the films, Campbell noted, "You know, I thought real art stopped with Picasso, Joyce and Mann. Now I know it hasn't."[42]

After his trilogy was complete, Lucas's goals seemed to be not so much about making films as financing his castle, Skywalker Ranch, which came to symbolize how far the young nerd from Modesto had truly come—or perhaps how far down he had fallen, depending on one's certain point of view. His marriage was over; his three films were complete, and his castle was created. His friends, such as Coppola, still lamented the direction his career had taken. He was a king now, but his battle with his subjects had not yet begun.

Among the kids who were at Disneyland on opening day was an eleven-year-old George Lucas. *Walt Disney Pictures/ Photofest © Walt Disney Pictures*

Star Tours employed military-grade flight simulators to give customers the feeling that they were flying through the *Star Wars* universe for four and a half minutes, engaging in dogfights with TIE Fighters, and attacking the Death Star. *Photofest*

One of George's favorite comics while growing up was Scrooge McDuck, a miserly venture capitalist who traveled around the world in search of riches. *Buena Vista Pictures/Photofest © Buena Vista Pictures*

The *Flash Gordon* serials, released by Universal in 1936, 1938, and 1940, were episodic and eventually aired in syndication on U.S. television in the 1950s, where they came to the attention of a young George Lucas. *Universal Pictures/ Photofest © Universal Pictures*

Lucas's first feature film, *THX 1138*, was based on a fifteen-minute short film that he made at USC called *Electronic Labyrinth THX 1138 4EB*. *Warner Bros./Photofest © Warner Bros.*

The dystopic nightmare of *THX 1138* carries its message of impending dehumanization by de-emphasizing dialogue and highlighting emotional stress as the film's protagonist, played by Robert Duvall, encounters nightmarish scenarios, including being imprisoned in endless white space and nearly being trampled by a stampede of commuting humans. *Warner Bros./Photofest © Warner Bros.*

The sexuality in *THX 1138* is devoid of eroticism, yet plays an important role in the film. *Warner Bros. Pictures/Photofest © Warner Bros Pictures*

*American Graffiti*, and in particular the character of Toad, provides tremendous insight into George Lucas's life as a teenager growing up in Modesto, California. *MCA/Universal Pictures/Photofest © Universal Pictures*

Despite Toad being a nerd in *American Graffiti*, he has the night of his life, getting the girl and taking part in an epic drag race. *MCA/Universal Pictures/Photofest* © *Universal Pictures*

*American Graffiti* celebrates the beauty of the cars as much, or more so, than the women. *Universal Pictures/Photofest* © *Universal Pictures*

From 1967 to 1972, a flurry of films by a group of fresh-faced, newly minted maverick directors ignited what the press soon began calling the New Hollywood. *AMPAS/Photofest © A.M.P.A.S.* *Photographer: Matt Petit*

*Jaws* and *Star Wars* marked the ultimate triumph of the B-movie. *Universal Pictures/ Photofest © Universal Pictures*

Ralph McQuarrie's sketches helped Lucas acquire a contract from Fox for *Star Wars*, more so than the script treatments. *Lucasfilm Ltd./Twentieth Century Fox Film Corp./Photofest © Lucasfilm Ltd./ Twentieth Century Fox Film Corp.*

George's inner circle mostly hated early sneak previews of *Star Wars*, including his wife, who told him his movie was for kids, whereas Scorcese's *New York, New York* was for grownups, and that nobody would take his film seriously. *Lucasfilm Ltd./ Twentieth Century Fox Film Corp./Photofest © Lucasfilm Ltd./ Twentieth Century Fox Film Corp.*

Lucas realized that Darth Vader was a strong villain, but he had no idea the character would be so popular. *Lucasfilm Ltd./Twentieth Century © Lucasfilm Ltd./Twentieth Century Fox Film Corp. Photographer: John Jay*

While George and Marcia sat at the Hamburger Hamlet having lunch on May 25, 1977, they noticed a huge commotion across the street at Mann's Chinese Theatre on Hollywood Boulevard. *Photofest*

George and Marcia traveled to New York for the premier of Scorsese's film, *New York, New York*. Scorsese blamed his movie's failure on *Star Wars*, noting bitterly that *Star Wars* had taken all the chips off the table, a charge that he would level again over four decades later. *Photofest*

Of all the *Star Wars* characters, Han Solo is likely the one whom Lucas most longed to be. *Lucasfilm Ltd./Twentieth Century © Lucasfilm Ltd./Twentieth Century Fox Film Corp.*

*Episode IV: The Empire Strikes Back* ends as a neutered Luke looks into space along with Leia who, unbeknownst to him, is really his sister. *TM Lucasfilm Ltd.*

Because of Vader's immense popularity, it became clear that he would have to play a much larger role in the subsequent films and that Lucas would need to expand on his mythology. *Twentieth Century Fox/Photofest © Twentieth Century Fox Film Corp.*

Louis, a quintessential nerd, has sex with the popular blonde cheerleader, demonstrating his sexual prowess and quipping at one point that jocks only think about sports while nerds only think about sex. *Revenge of the Nerds*, like *American Graffiti*, is a nerd fantasy. *Twentieth Century Fox/Photofest © Twentieth Century Fox Film Corp.*

From the moment *Star Wars* came out, its fandom refused to stay in its lane. In many cases, because of negative stereotypes, fans have not been a trusted component in the entertainment equation. *NBC/Photofest © NBC*

The most controversial alteration that Lucas made, according to fans, and one that clearly altered the character arc of Han Solo, perhaps the most beloved character in the entire franchise, involved the scene between Han and Greedo in the cantina on Mos Eisley. *20th Century Fox Pictures/Photofest © 20th Century Fox*

One of the major new scenes in the 1997 Special Edition of *Star Wars: A New Hope* involved Han Solo encountering Jabba the Hut in Mos Eisley, a scene inconsequential to the film and roundly criticized by fans. *Lucasfilm Ltd./Twentieth Century © Lucasfilm Ltd./Twentieth Century Fox Film Corp.*

*Star Trek* slash fiction was not all that removed from the canonical episodes. *NBC/Photofest © NBC*

Lucas thought that digital technology would quickly and cheaply make up for whatever the story lacked. *Lucasfilm Ltd./20th Century Fox/Photofest © Lucasfilm Ltd.*

Whether he was too young, too cute, or simply the speaker of bad dialogue, the responses to the performance of a young Darth Vader were merciless and never-ending, so much so that Jake Lloyd quit acting after his role in *The Phantom Menace*. *Lucasfilm Ltd./20th Century Fox/Photofest* © *Lucasfilm Ltd. Photographer: Keith Hamshere*

Samuel L. Jackson made several public appeals to Lucas for any role—no matter how small—even the role of an anonymous Stormtrooper. *Lucasfilm/Photofest* © *Lucasfilm Ltd.*

Fans attacked scenes involving the romance between Anakin and Padme, describing them as over-the-top and cheesy. *Lucasfilm Ltd./Photofest* © *Lucasfilm Ltd.*

The Clones are the most tragic figures in the *Star Wars* universe, and their story arc in *The Clone Wars* is the best in the series. *Lucasfilm Ltd./Photofest* © *Lucasfilm Ltd.*

Lucas was especially helpful when it came to stories about the Clones themselves. *Lucasfilm Ltd./Photofest © Lucasfilm Ltd.*

In the documentary *The People vs George Lucas* (2010), fans outright compared Lucas to both Darth Vader and Luke Skywalker. *Exhibit A Pictures/Photofest © Exhibit A Pictures*

Lucas likened watching Disney *Star Wars* films to attending his child's wedding and having to deal with his ex-wife. *Celebrity Productions/Photofest © Celebrity Productions*

Lucas reassured the public that he was confident that under Kathleen Kennedy's leadership and the aegis of Disney, *Star Wars* would live on for generations to come. Passing the *Star Wars* franchise on to a new generation of filmmakers under Disney's control would prove to be harder than anyone thought. *Warner Bros. Pictures/ Photofest © Warner Bros. Pictures*

In a nod to fans of the original trilogy, Filoni based all his concept art for Rebels on the paintings and sketches of Ralph McQuarrie. *Disney XD/Photofest © Disney XD*

Lucas criticized *The Force Awakens* as being a throwback movie that expressly catered to the fans. *Walt Disney Studios Motion Pictures/Photofest © Walt Disney Studios Motion Pictures*

Director Gareth Edward's vision for *Rogue One* was for it to be a gritty, documentary-style war film, which just so happened to be George Lucas's identical vision for the original *Star Wars*. *Walt Disney Studios Motion Pictures/Photofest © Walt Disney Studios Motion Pictures*

Whether due to *Star Wars* fatigue or the shuffling of directors, *Solo* was the least successful *Star Wars* movie of all time. *Walt Disney Studios Motion Pictures/Photofest © Walt Disney Studios Motion Pictures*

In subverting the expectations of fans, Rian Johnson also subverted the expectations of the film's biggest star, Mark Hamill. This alone was reason enough for fans to hate *The Last Jedi* even more than the prequels. *Walt Disney Studios Motion Pictures/Photofest © Walt Disney Studios Motion Pictures*

*The Mandalorian* protagonist, Din Djarin, owes a huge debt to the first *Star Wars* Mandalorian, Boba Fett, who rose to stardom in the first trilogy despite limited screen time and an unceremonious ending in *Return of the Jedi* when he seemingly dies in the Sarlacc Pit in the Tatooine desert. *Twentieth Century Fox Film Corp./Photofest © Twentieth Century Fox Film Corp.*

Almost immediately after *The Mandalorian* premiered, memes of Baby Yoda popped up all over the internet. Never mind that there was no plausible way the baby could actually be Yoda, who is 900 years old in *Return of the Jedi* and dies on screen. *Lucasfilm Ltd./20th Century Fox/ ©Lucasfilm, Ltd. Photographer: Terry Chostner*

Grimy Stormtroopers and ruthless bounty hunters, some of whom were first introduced in *The Empire Strikes Back*, populate *The Mandalorian. Lucasfilm Ltd./20th Century Fox/Photofest © Lucasfilm Ltd./20th Century Fox*

*The Rise of Skywalker* was an apology for the much superior preceding film, *The Last Jedi*. In trying to win back fans who hated *The Last Jedi*, Abrams and Lucasfilm Disney laid an egg. *Walt Disney Studios Motion Pictures/Photofest © Walt Disney Studios Motion Pictures*

We might look at *Star Wars* fandom as representative of Luke Skywalker, a true nerd son responsible for Vader's destruction and redemption. *Lucasfilm Ltd./20th Century Fox © Lucasfilm, Ltd. Photographer: Terry Chostner*

# 4

# A GREAT DISTURBANCE IN THE FORCE

L ucas invented a history for Skywalker Ranch, similar to the invented history that he created for himself and the *Star Wars* franchise. The fabricated history held that the land had been used for a monastery until a retired sea captain bought it in 1869. In the 1880s, the story went, the captain tried his hand at winemaking and built a brick winery. Through the ensuing decades, descendants built a library and guesthouses. Lucas wished to give the impression of old money, another way to secure his place among the landed gentry, firmly situated within the culture not as a marginalized nerd who had trouble with the ladies, but as an American prince famous throughout the world, a pop-culture prophet with religious significance.[1] The apocryphal monastic history of the ranch also invoked a sexual asceticism in line with Lucas's preferences.

Eventually Lucas devoted a bunker to surveillance equipment, and guests had to check in at multiple checkpoints to enter the compound. Lucas always maintained that Skywalker Ranch would be a filmmaking enterprise where he and his filmmaking buddies, as well as other enterprising filmmakers, could make small personal films in a supportive and creative environment with state-of-the-art facilities. Despite Lucas's best intentions, his old friends grew worried that his vision had transformed from a filmmaking oasis to a private empire where Lucas could wage complete control.[2]

At one of his annual cookouts, old friend John Milius recalled thinking of Lucas as a cult of personality, as he watched workers usher guests along a roped-off section outside, offering suggestions about where to stand to catch a glimpse of George. Milius joked that if George began offering Kool-Aid to guests, he was "gonna bail"—a reference to Jim Jones and his People's Temple cult in Jonestown, Guyana, which made headlines in 1978 when cult members committed mass suicide at Jones's behest. Jones insisted that his followers drink cyanide-laced Kool-Aid, after which he killed himself by a self-inflicted gunshot to the head.[3]

Unlike Coppola who, when he was on top, bought a building in San Francisco, a theater, a Learjet, and a newspaper—all of which he mortgaged when *Apocalypse Now* ran into financial trouble—Lucas was more interested in creative freedom and the ability to finance his own movies. All his money went into Skywalker Ranch, which actually depended on the proceeds from his films as well as merchandising. When both Coppola and Lucas sat down for an interview together, both were asked what they would do if they were given $2 billion. Coppola immediately said he would borrow another $2 billion and buy a city. Lucas responded by saying he would invest a billion and with the remaining billion buy a town.[4]

In the 1980s, after his trilogy was complete, Lucas found himself in court on more than one occasion, defending his franchise. In March 1983, President Ronald Reagan proposed his Strategic Defense Initiative. Part of the initiative included a space-based weapons system that was capable of blasting incoming nuclear missiles out of the sky. Senator Ted Kennedy referred to the boondoggle effort pejoratively as "Star Wars." The media soon picked up the nickname, and Star Wars began to be used interchangeably with SDI in reference to the defense plan. Soon, competing political commercials about the initiative were using the term. Lucas went ballistic. He argued that the use of "Star Wars" in relation to the SDI, whether for or against, was an infringement on his trademark. He also did not want his franchise associated with a noxious subject like nuclear holocaust.[5] Lucas lost the case. Judge Gerhard A. Gesell, the same judge who presided over many of the Watergate trials, cited non-trade use of the term "Star Wars," arguing that Lucas had no right to prevent the use of the term among politicians and the media.[6] Lucas's concern for the reputation of his franchise, his fear of association with something that he felt might taint his product, drove him to protect his brand against everything from rap groups to particular types of fan fiction called "slash fiction" that featured same-sex relationships between his characters.

In 1990, Lucas sued rap star Luther Campbell of 2 Live Crew for calling himself Luke Skywalker. Lucas was awarded $300,000 from Campbell, and the MC was ordered to cease using the name. 2 Live Crew earned a reputation for pushing the envelope when it came to obscenity laws, particularly on their album *As Nasty As They Wanna Be*, and their song "Me So Horny," which came to the attention of Christian groups such as the American Family Association, who soon filed an obscenity suit against the rap group and won. The suit was eventually overturned, but Lucas wanted no part of this feud. He wanted nothing to do with sex in relation to his movies, and he particularly did not want his franchise anywhere near an obscenity case or to be associated with a rap group that performed songs like "The Fuck Shop." Luther Campbell never forgave Lucas for the lawsuit and was particularly upset about having to relinquish $300,000 to the famed director.

Lucas found it increasingly difficult to control his fandom. For example, *Return of the Jedi* had quite an effect on a young man in Milwaukee by the name of Jeffrey Dahmer. Dahmer was particularly taken with the emperor and his power to control mortals. Dahmer watched the film several times a week during the height of his killing spree. The film so entranced him, especially the character of the emperor, that he bought yellow-tinted contact lenses and wore them when he went to the bars in which he predated his victims, most of them young black men.[7]

Coppola once referred to Lucas as a single mother. Lucas told the *New York Times*, "There's no one I admire more than single mothers . . . because they are the real heroes."[8] Lucas backed up his pronouncement by implementing family-friendly policies in his companies and on Skywalker Ranch, so much so that *Working Mother* magazine named Lucas a "Family Champion," an honor bestowed on employers whose policies supported working parents, especially working mothers. *Working Mother* also named Lucasfilm one of the best companies to work for, listing benefits such as child-care centers, flexible work schedules, paid leave for employees who had sick family members, and insurance for domestic partners and their dependents. Lucas noted that he too was a single parent of three, offering, "I guess I qualify as a working mother." By all accounts, employees were generally happy working for Lucas. "I find myself with this little country," he observed. "It's got about 2,000 citizens and they are very complex."[9] Over the years, Lucas claimed to be an ordinary everyman who just happened to have accidentally become rich, once noting, "I'm so ordinary that a lot of people can relate to me, because it's the same kind of ordinary that they are . . . I think it gives me an insight into the mass audience. I know what I liked as a kid, and I still like it."[10] Lucas's claims to ordinariness were a little disingenuous, given his white male privilege as well as his upper-middle-class upbringing.

Lucas's political views were generally liberal except on issues like crime and unemployment. He favored maximum prison sentences and disfavored welfare. He was essentially anti-intellectual but managed an extremely sophisticated multimillion-dollar company. He was one part ruthless dictator and one part single mother.

One of George's favorite comics when growing up was Scrooge McDuck, featuring the titular miserly venture capitalist who travels around the world in search of riches. This love of Scrooge McDuck informed George's vision for Indiana Jones. Scrooge was the uncle of Donald Duck and had his own comic called *Walt Disney's Uncle Scrooge*. Scrooge's schemes often enriched him. Lucas once noted, "To me, Uncle Scrooge . . . is a perfect indicator of the American psyche. . . . There's so much that is precisely the essence of America about him that it's staggering."[11] Lucas bought a page of Carl Barks's original art for an *Uncle Scrooge* comic. A less innocent view of Scrooge is that he is a money-grubbing imperialist who stops at nothing to amass his fortune, a sort of economic psychopath white supremacist. Uncle Scrooge is generally an odd character for a young man to idolize.

From the beginning, the *Star Wars* experience included a certain level of masochism and tension on the part of fans. Part of the *Star Wars* experience was literally waiting in extremely long lines to see the latest *Star Wars* movie. These lines were dreadfully uncomfortable, and yet fans did not think twice about enduring them. They wanted to wait in these lines. The long lines were part of the experience. The catch was that, inherent in this tacit exchange, was the expectation that the waiting and the pain would be worth it. The long lines positioned the fans in a subservient role. They were worshipers willing to make long and arduous treks to religious sites in order to experience their God. They were willing to sleep outdoors, to commune with one another, to adopt an identity all in honor of George Lucas's creation.

The first *Star Wars* convention took place at the Stouffer Concourse Hotel in Los Angeles in May 1987. Over 9,000 fans, many dressed in character, poured into the hotel. For three days of events, the price was $18 a ticket. Fans could buy merchandise and memorabilia. Lucas stunned the audience by showing up on the last evening and taking questions. By 1987 Lucas was still not totally cognizant of the strength and power of his own fandom, especially fan fiction writers.

Fan fiction, also known as fanfic, is fictional writing created by fans and inspired by the objects of their interest, often films or television shows. Fanfic can be divided into several categories, such as AU or alternative universe, which employs canonical characters in noncanonical plots; genfic, or general-interest fiction; RPF, which stands for real-person fiction that fictionalizes the lives of celebrities; darkfic, a category that contains graphic violence; cross-universe stories in which, for example, Doctor Who might appear in the *Star Trek* or *Star Wars* universes; and slash fiction, a lesser-known form that explores same-sex relationships between characters.[12]

Fan fiction also appears in other industries, like music. For example, pop-slash or rockfic is popular among music fans and often features stories about famous musicians interacting with each other or with fans. Fanfic is most popular among fans of films and television shows, however. Fanfic can function as an extension of canonical films, texts, or as parody and subversion. Fans do not universally accept fanfic. Fans can use fanfic as a way to comment on canonical texts, instigating trouble in the larger film and television communities.

The word canon refers to texts that represent the best a genre has to offer, the cream of the crop. Over the last several decades, the idea of canonicity has come under fire in academic circles as a dated designation stemming from an era in which critics and other appointed guardians of elite culture operated un-challenged in their educational roles. In university literature courses, race and gender theorists have challenged the prevalence of dead white men populating the reading lists making up the canon, charging that the literary canon has been a product of racism and discrimination. What cultural gatekeepers deem as the cream of the crop vis-à-vis literature is fluid and always changing. Gatekeepers have ousted and reinstated writers such as Ernest Hemingway and Zora Neale Hurston. With regard to films and television shows, canon refers to the original films and television shows on which a fandom is based. Additionally, the term canon can also apply to products licensed by the producers of the original texts, such as books, comics, games, and television shows.

Producers of canonical texts have a difficult time responding to fanfic. On one hand, they view it as a marginal or unlicensed activity, but on the other hand, they view it as evidence of fan enthusiasm, something they do not want to undermine since fan enthusiasm often translates into profit for producers. From the point of view of fans, fanfic provides creative freedom and fosters fan com-munities. Fans celebrate the universes by molding them to fit their desires and whims. They reimagine characters and scenes and expand on minor characters or glossed-over events that take place offstage. Fanfic allows fans to become more invested in the story and characters.

Sometimes fanfic is a product of the insatiable hunger of consumers, espe-cially if a show has been canceled, or a film franchise has gone dormant. Fans simply want more stories in these worlds and create stories themselves instead of waiting for producers to create them. The tension lies in the multifaceted com-plexity of fan fiction. On one hand, fan culture functions as free advertising and a testament to the popularity of commercial media. On the other hand, fan work has the power to damage public perceptions of cultural artifacts and reduce profits by offering the product for free. Media organizations have a wide array of methods for responding to fanfic, including doing nothing, or using legal means to prevent the dissemination of fan work.

The amicable relationship between Lucasfilm and fan fiction writers ended at some point in the 1980s when Lucas received a story wherein Darth Vader rapes Han Solo. Lucas was so aghast at the story that he ordered the entire fanzine shut down. Most same-sex relationships in fan fiction do not involve sexual violence. The raping of Han Solo by Darth Vader was not indicative of the kind of same-sex stories popular in fanfic. Nevertheless, after this occurrence, Lucasfilm took a hard line on fanzines, especially stories that violated the family values of the original films. One letter to a fanzine read:

> Lucasfilm Ltd does own all rights to the *Star Wars* characters and we are going to insist upon no pornography. This may mean no fanzines if that measure is what is necessary to stop the few from darkening the reputation our company is so proud of . . . since all of the *Star Wars* saga is PG rated, any story those publishers do print should also be PG. Lucasfilm does not produce any X-rated *Star Wars* episodes, so why should we be placed in a light where people think we do? . . . You don't own these characters and can't publish anything about them without our permission.[13]

Most fans of *Star Wars* were not aware that there were X-rated *Star Wars* stories available in fanzines. This was not a widespread cottage industry that significantly affected the reputation of *Star Wars*. Even if fans were aware of the existence of fanzines that included stories of a sexual or even homosexual nature, it was very unlikely that these fans ascribed their origins to Lucasfilm or thought they were canon. The question was really about ownership of the characters, and that became blurry when fans immediately began taking part in the franchise through the toys and costumes, creating their own stories and expanding the narrative possibilities of the *Star Wars* universe. The letter's emphasis on pornographic fanfic subtly evoked Lucas's strange and complicated relationship with sex that dogged his adolescence and his marriage as well as many of his films. It was clear that Lucas was not a sex-positive person and was highly insecure about sex and sexuality in general, and this was why he reacted so strongly to fanfiction that included sexual activity among his characters.

One popular narrative is that slash fiction originated within the *Star Trek* franchise among fans who simply wanted more *Star Trek* stories and did not care where they got them. The prevalence of slash stories, as the story went, ultimately reflected negatively on the *Star Trek* franchise and debased the brand. George Lucas was apparently aware of this and preempted the co-opting of his franchise by fans who wrote stories involving same-sex relationships among his characters by handpicking a few writers and allowing them to create officially sanctioned *Star Wars* stories. The hope was that the stories that became known as the Extended Universe, or EU, would leave little market share or cultural space for slash stories.[14]

Like genfic, its heterosexual counterpart, slash fiction uses the canonical texts and films as context for stories that attempt to fill in the blanks the movies created, blanks that involve a deeper look at relationships among characters such as Luke and his buddy Biggs. Authors of slash fiction have often been secretive of their work, choosing to use pseudonyms and *noms de plume* rather than their real names. Lucasfilm drew strong distinctions between authorized and unauthorized texts and outright forbade slash fiction. The pen names of the authors insulated them from potential lawsuits, or at the very least cease-and-desist letters that threatened litigation. Because Lucas failed to explore in any real-life way the sex lives of the characters, these became fecund gaps for fans to fill. Slash writers simply felt as though they were revealing the homoerotic subtext just under the surface. Lucas's reaction was textbook homophobia, likely drawn from his own sexual insecurities.

*Star Wars* slash fiction writers have mostly been women. For some women, writing slash fiction is no doubt a sexual turn-on. Others are interested in exploring alternative forms of masculinity. One of the few men who writes *Star Wars* slash fiction once noted that it is similar to playing with the toys as a young man.[15] Many slash writers suggest that they are not interested in improving Lucas's vision with their slash fiction. They simply wish to take characters in a different direction.

Due to the hard line that Lucasfilm took with slash fiction, the adult-oriented stories went underground and were only distributed among a group of interested folks. The threat from Lucasfilm was effective and long-lasting. Even contemporary owners of websites where slash fiction is published are a little skittish. Lucasfilm went after publishers of slash fiction aggressively in the 1980s, and webmasters are still a little worried. One webmistress noted that decades of threats and legal action on the part of Lucasfilm still causes skittishness among fan makers.[16]

In popular genres in decades past, intense male relationships were very common and slashers simply took these relationships a step further. What participatory fandom was most guilty of was not being passive consumers of cultural texts. Their lack of passivity caused conflicts between themselves and the cultural producers, including Lucas and Lucasfilm. Fan culture confronted popular standards of reading, especially in relation to *Star Wars*.

The term "slash" originally denoted the two characters on which a particular story focused, such as Kirk/Spock or K/S in the *Star Trek* franchise. The term also suggested that the story involved same-sex erotic relationships. Usually the term slash referred to same-sex relationships among characters who were widely believed to be heterosexual or who, in the world of the created universe, were definitely heterosexual. Often slash stories attempted to play with these expectations and subvert them as part of the fun. Oftentimes the predicaments of the characters that triggered their same-sex sexual activity did nothing to undermine their essential heterosexuality.

The genre has always been controversial in fan communities. Many felt it crossed the line and undermined the original artifact and characterizations. Those who felt this way missed the point of slash. The alteration of established characterization is not a transgression as much as it is the point of the creative exercise. Slash relies on the unwavering masculinity of the characters within the canonical universe as a way of steaming the story. Without the uncompromising sexuality of the characters, slash stories would not be as powerful. In a 1977 essay, Kendra Hunter accused slash writers of character rape and assessed slash writing as inherently bad writing, since the tropes were necessarily out of character.[17] Fan communities treated slash writers as second-class fans and pariahs, often banning their work at cons for fear of offending personnel attached to the television shows or films.

Since the 1970s and 1980s, slash has moved on from *Star Trek* to include *Starsky and Hutch*, *Miami Vice*, *Simon and Simon* and, of course, *Star Wars*. One example of a slash story involving Kirk/Spock imagines the two men stranded on a desert planet with a bleak chance of rescue or survival. Their ship, the Enterprise, is on an emergency mission to deliver a plague antidote to Mmyrrmyon II. While stranded on an island, Spock contracts Pon Farr, a Vulcan mating fever. In order to avoid certain death, Spock must ejaculate. Kirk realizes that the only way to save Spock's life is to help his friend orgasm. Masturbation is evidently out of the question for Spock. Kirk convinces himself that helping his friend orgasm is the proper path to take as a friend and the captain of the starship Enterprise. Spock, on the other hand, resents Kirk's proposed intervention as a violation of his privacy. Nevertheless, he reluctantly agrees, and both he and Kirk achieve release. After the two return to the Enterprise, Kirk finds his new erotic homosexual fantasies disturbing compared to his typical ones involving blue-skinned Andorian women.

This story appears in Gayle Feyrer's Cosmic Fuck series.[18] As the series unfolds, both Kirk and Spock develop their newfound non-normative sexuality and their strong sexual feelings for one another. Eventually they include Dr. McCoy in a friendly ménage à trois. The Cosmic Fuck series is typical of the slash genre in its expansion of traditional masculinity to include same-sex relationships. In the case of Kirk, Spock, and Dr. McCoy, their same-sex activity does not change their abilities to function as space explorers and members of the Enterprise. To someone like George Lucas, whose sexuality and sense of himself as a man was a constant source of insecurity since he was a young child, this sort of idea must have been terrifying.

In slash fiction, traditional masculinity is the focus of the text with regard to how conventional or hegemonic masculinities create obstacles for intimate male relationships. Slash fiction often focuses on hypermasculine characters who have never had the opportunity to express their latent homosexuality or to enjoy close relationships with men. This is why the characters in slash fiction are usually straight men. The dramatization of breaking taboos is the conflict of the story.

The machinations of this tension rely on male characters' fear of being unmasked as anything other than masculine. The male characters dare not express their feelings to any other character for fear of violent reprisal. This quintessential homophobia harkens back to notions of homosexual panic, which was at one time a legitimate defense for hate crimes against homosexuals. The characters in slash fiction often consider the repercussions of letting their guard down regarding their strict straight sexuality as well as their own self-assessment of their masculinity. They consider their professional status, their status with their families and friends, and often shudder to think what the consequences might be should they act on their same-sex desires.

These are the emotional equations at play with regard to the intensity of homophobia in our culture, and an equation with which George Lucas was likely familiar in one way or another, as he was always extremely reluctant to delve into matters of sexuality in his films at all, especially after his first feature films *THX 1138* and *American Graffiti*. It is therefore no wonder that Lucas reacted so intensely when he happened upon a slash story that involved Darth Vader and Han Solo, an occurrence that forever changed the course of Lucasfilm's response to fandom.

In some cases, canonized material is not that far removed from overt slash material. In a 1968 episode of *Star Trek* titled "Plato's Stepchildren," Kirk, Spock, and Dr. McCoy respond to a distress signal from a distant planet. When they arrive, they find a people who have fashioned a republic based on the teachings of Plato.[19] They are nearly immortal and at one time eugenically trimmed their numbers to thirty-eight in order to form a utopia. The Platonians have a telekinetic power with which they can control objects with their minds, all except a slave court jester dwarf named Alexander. Alexander is enamored with Kirk because Kirk is clearly strong despite not having the power of telekinesis. When the Dwarf asks Kirk whether there are other powerless dwarfs on his planet, the captain tells him that where they are from, size, shape, and color do not matter.

When Kirk takes issue with not being able to leave the planet, Parmen, the leader of the Platonians, forces Kirk to smack himself repeatedly. The sadistic dynamics in the story evoke a culture of BDSM among the Platonians. Despite the evidence that the Platonians have fashioned more of a fascist regime than a democratic republic, Parmen insists to Kirk that they have created the most democratic republic conceivable. When Kirk rebukes the philosopher king, Parmen says that in Kirk's culture justice is enforced by technological power whereas among Platonians, mental power rules.

In order to force Dr. McCoy to stay on Platonius as their medical doctor, Parmen threatens the rest of the crew and makes fools out of Kirk and Spock by forcing them to dance against their will. Parmen then forces Spock, an emotionless Vulcan, to laugh and cry while Alexander rides Kirk like a horse as he kicks and neighs. Kirk's degradation smacks of sado-masochism. When two female crewmembers of the Enterprise are beamed down to Platonius alongside Kirk, Spock, and Dr. McCoy, the episode transforms into a narrative about sex, sexual desire, and sexual taboo. Parmen forces the four members of the Enterprise to put on a show for the thirty-eight Platonians, including compelling Spock to serenade the audience. Spock's forcible expressions of emotion and song undermine his masculinity as a Vulcan in the same way slash fiction seeks to explore new versions of masculinity among popular characters. Kirk's humiliation also compromises his powerful masculinity as the leader of the Enterprise. The forced behaviors of Kirk and Spock are a form of torture undergirding the strict parameters of their masculinity. If Spock could express his emotions and feel free to enjoy singing, and if Kirk could be a little more playful, perhaps they would be happier men. The notion that these forced behaviors are painful and torturous points to the strict rules of traditional masculinity to which Kirk and Spock adhere.

In the second act of the performance, Parmen forces the members of the Enterprise to interact with each another sexually. Parmen couples off the men and women heterosexually, but the threat of homosexual coupling lurks just under the surface, especially since the Platonians are interested in humiliating the men by undermining their masculinity. This possibility positions the episode as latently slash. When Parmen forces Kirk and Lieutenant Uhura, a brown-skinned African American woman, to kiss, Parmen breaks extratextual taboos, since the kiss represents the first interracial kiss on television and wound up garnering much controversy. Lieutenant Uhura expresses her lust for Kirk, who then brandishes a whip and whips her, evocative of racial slavery and the raping of black slave women by white masters. Kirk and Spock soon gain control of the situation by acquiring the telekinetic power with the help of Dr. McCoy and eventually escape, but the episode represents a viable narrative for a classic slash story.

By the mid-1980s, Skywalker Ranch was complete. The staff operated under strict rules when it came to their boss: Do not approach George. Do not chat up George. Should George start a conversation, keep to work-related topics. Skywalker Ranch included the main house as well as several other buildings. Filmmakers could complete all pre- and postproduction necessary for a film at Skywalker Ranch. Though the facilities would never be truly finished, Lucas announced that the ranch was open for business.

# 5

# I AM ALTERING THE DEAL

On the morning of November 1, 1994, dressed in his everyman outfit of jeans, plaid shirt, and white sneakers, George Lucas returned to the universe that had laid cinematically dormant for the last decade. Clearly aware of the historical moment and his importance as a filmmaker, Lucas invited a camera crew to his home. Lucas wearily confided into the camera that his daughter had been sick the night before and that he had not gotten much sleep. At his desk in the upstairs office of his San Anselmo home, Lucas brought out his preferred long yellow legal pad, the very kind that he used to write *A New Hope*.

Lucas invited a writer from *Variety* magazine to Skywalker Ranch to tell the world that he was ready to return to the *Star Wars* saga. He had become inextricable from the franchise that made him rich and famous. He intended to shoot *Episodes I*, *II*, and *III* all at once and release them a few years apart. He was already pessimistic about the prequels even before writing the first word, noting, "For every person who loves *Episode I*, there will be two or three who hate it. . . . You just never know with these things. . . . You can destroy these things. It is possible."[1] These words would prove prophetic.

The driving forces behind Lucas's return to the *Star Wars* universe were many. First, he still needed to fund Skywalker Ranch. Second, he wanted to reclaim the throne of master creator. Third, Lucas believed the technology had finally caught up to his vision. No longer were puppets and rubber suits necessary. The director always felt constrained by what was technologically possible, even though many fans felt like the innovations required under the constraints inspired rather than compromised his genius.

Computer-generated imagery, or CGI, had developed over the years to the point where Lucas felt he could get exactly what he wanted. In 1992, Spielberg optioned Michael Crichton's book *Jurassic Park* and hired one of the few remaining special effects engineers from the original *Star Wars*, Dennis Muren, to work on the film. Spielberg realized that the look of the dinosaurs was key to the success of the film. He had huge problems with the shark in *Jaws* that forced him to create drama and tension without actually showing the shark to the audience. He did not want to recreate this innovation in *Jurassic Park*, even though it was a good example of a filmmaker working under constraints that ultimately made the film better.

When Muren invited Spielberg and Lucas to see what he had been working on, both filmmakers were amazed when they saw life-like dinosaurs running across the frame. Lucas noted, "everyone had tears in their eyes. . . . We may have reached a level here where we actually artificially created reality, which is of course what movies were trying to do all along."[2] This was a notable observation from Lucas. From the beginning, Lucas had very different goals from his American New Wave contemporaries, such as Martin Scorcese and Brian De Palma, whose gritty hyperrealism exposed the underbelly of the American dream. Lucas was more interested in creating alternate realities that masked his shortcomings. Lucas's claim that he cried when he saw some of the dailies for *Jurassic Park* is a perfect synecdoche of his emotional makeup. What Lucas *really* cared about deeply, what could bring him to tears, what could touch his soul, was technology.

Lucas later added, "I didn't want to go back and write one of these movies unless I had the technology available to really tell the kind of story I was interested in telling . . . I wanted to be able to explore the world I'd created to its fullest. So I waited until I had the technological means to do that."[3]

Lucas was also aware that *Star Wars* fandom was clamoring for new films, a frenzy that Lucas instigated by numbering the extant films IV through VI, implying that the first three installments were already conceived. Lucas noted, "Part of the reason for doing it . . . is that it's the first question I get asked. Not this is who I am or anything, but when are you going to do the next *Star Wars*? So if I do the next ones, hopefully people will introduce themselves first."[4]

If there were no technological constraints in producing *Episodes I, II,* and *III,* there *were* narrative constraints, since the first three films were prequels to the existing three films. The plot of the extant three films boxed Lucas in narratively. Darth Vader had taken over the franchise, and it was his story Lucas needed to tell. Early on, Lucas realized that the prequels would center on Anakin's turn to the dark side, the primary narrative development in the *Star Wars* saga and one that mirrored Lucas's own transformation from nerd to overlord.

Lucas and his team spent eighteen months working on the character Jar Jar Binks, introducing him in the initial draft as a character who spoke standard English. It was not until later drafts that Lucas changed Jar Jar into a buffoon who spoke broken English. Lucas cast an African American actor, Ahmed Best, to play the role, opening himself up to charges of minstrelsy, a nineteenth-century form of entertainment that employed racist caricatures of black people who were mostly played by white people. Lucas argued that he based the character on the great silent film comedic actors like Buster Keaton and Charlie Chaplin. Nevertheless, Jar Jar wound up being a great source of pain for the director, forcing him to limit the character's role in the subsequent films.

Early in the process, Michael Jackson contacted Lucas and told him that he was interested in playing Jar Jar. Jackson wanted to play the role in full makeup and rubber suit rather than have Lucas create the character using CGI. The two had already worked together on *Captain EO*, a science fiction film shown at Disney theme parks in the 1980s, but Lucas politely declined, sticking to his original plan to create digitally the most hated character in the *Star Wars* universe.[5]

In 1995, Hasbro, which had absorbed Kenner, produced a new line of *Star Wars* toys called "The Power of the Force." Toy managers right away noticed there were more adults than kids buying the toys, an indication that the folks Lucas had to win over were the squeaky-wheeled adults for whom the originals were a religion. By 1996, largely due to the revenue from merchandising, Lucas owned 2,500 acres of land on and around Skywalker Ranch and was negotiating for more.

At a dinner for director and producer Arthur Penn in 1996, also attended by filmmaker Mathew Robbins, the celebrated Penn held court and broached his film *Little Big Man*. The director discussed the vagaries of filmmaking and the expediencies required that are out of the filmmaker's control. For example, Penn brought up the fact that while filming *Little Big Man*, a shift in the weather melted all the snow, and the film crew had to wait a month for more to fall. Lucas responded to the anecdote by suggesting, "That's the difference between then and now. . . . If we were in that situation now, we could simply add snow in with CGI."[6] Penn responded with horror, indicating that Lucas had missed his point about making do with constraints as part of the filmmaking process. Lucas was completely serious about what he thought CGI could do. In fact, Lucas was eager to test out the new technology not on his *new* films but rather on the *original* films.

Lucas's rationale for changing the original films was that he was simply fixing problems that had dogged him from the beginning, problems that were now solvable with CGI. He felt his films were his to do with what he wished. It was like the roller coaster in his back yard, or the haunted house in his garage; they were his, and that was it. The mistake that he made was thinking he owned them in every sense of the word. Legally he could do whatever he wanted with his films, his artifacts, his cultural production; but ethically, there were millions of fans who felt *Star Wars* was theirs, and mucking with the original works was akin to stealing from their souls.

Lucas also suggested that he wanted to change the films for his son Jett, but Lucas and Muren had discussed how they might "update" the original films as early as 1993, before Jett was born.[7] When Lucas returned to the negatives of the old films, he was very upset to find that they had completely deteriorated, especially *A New Hope*, which was very dirty and scratched. Lucas and his team needed to restore the negatives before they could alter anything.

For Lucas, the original films only represented about 25 percent of his total vision. Lucas and Muren discussed altering nearly one hundred shots. The two would update the films, including the negatives and sound, and release the new versions as special editions. By the time Lucas released the special editions, he and his team had altered 277 shots of the original film. There were minor changes such as screen wipes, semi-minor changes such as the blinking dianoga in the trash compactor, and seventeen completely new shots. One of the major new scenes involved Han Solo encountering Jabba the Hut in Mos Eisley, a scene inconsequential to the entire film and roundly criticized by fans.

The most controversial change that Lucas made, according to fans—and one that clearly altered the character arc of Han Solo, perhaps the most beloved character in the entire franchise with the exception of Darth Vader—involved the scene between Han and Greedo in the cantina on Mos Eisley. In the original script, Greedo confronts Han with a drawn blaster, suggesting that Greedo is there to either capture Han or kill him. Unbeknownst to Greedo, Han has his own blaster pointed at Greedo under the table. The script notes, "Suddenly the slimy alien disappears in a blinding flash of light. Han pulls his smoking gun from beneath the table as the other patrons look on in bemused amazement. Han gets up and starts out of the cantina, flipping the bartender some coins as he leaves."[8] This scene solidifies Han Solo as a pirate who is not above killing an adversary in cold blood to save his hide. The scene gives the character an edge that fans adored. Lucas changed the scene and made Greedo shoot Han first, his shot just missing Han's head and exploding on the wall. The altered scene implies that Han's shot was really in self-defense, something quite different from the original script. Lucas would again change the shot after fans bemoaned the alteration, moving Greedo's shot up eleven frames so that both nearly shoot at the same time. Fans were not pacified. Lucas would tease fans throughout his life by wearing a T-shirt on multiple occasions that read "Han Shot First." He was not beyond antagonizing his fans. He still felt in control. This feeling would not last. There was always an element of playfulness when it came to Lucas's relationship with his fans, until the prequels soured the relationship completely.

Gunning down Greedo creates a character arc in which Han transforms from a murderous spicerunner pirate who would kill to get himself out of a jam to a hero rebel who fights for the light side of the force. By mitigating Han's ruthlessness in the cantina, Lucas weakened Han's character and his story arc. Lucas maintained that Greedo had always shot first, and that it was just the limitations of the film that made it seem like Han shot first. If this was the case, then the accident was a happy one that fans loved, and Lucas revising it weakened the overall film.

When all was said and done, the restoration cost Lucas around $10 million for four and one-half minutes of revised material, slightly more than the studio cut from his first two films. As for the originals, Lucas noted, "The original *Star Wars* was a joke, technically. . . . We did a lot of work, but there is nothing that I would like to do more than go back and redo all the special effects. . . . There were things I had to compromise on that weren't the way I really wanted them to be."[9] For *Star Wars* fans, the original trilogy was no joke, and the idea of Lucas returning to the originals and mucking with them was horrifying.

Adding insult to injury for *Star War* fans, Lucas doubled down on his alterations by hiding the original negatives of the original trilogy on Skywalker Ranch and refusing to show them. To Lucas, the originals did not exist. This was the straw that broke the camel's back for *Star Wars* fandom, a back Lucas needed covered for the upcoming prequels.

In the past, Lucas sparred with writers of fan fiction and even with other filmmakers who set films within the *Star Wars* universe. Some fans felt *Return of the Jedi* was a little too childish, especially the Ewoks of Endor. There were moans and gripes before, but nothing on the order of what occurred when Lucas changed the original films and then acted as though these originals did not exist. These were the films that fans knew and loved. Lucas was messing with something that was deeply important to fans. Lucas was mucking with a mythology. He had created a myth, then pulled the rug out from under a culture that had adopted that myth completely. This was a betrayal. This was unforgivable. This was an ill-advised path for Lucas to tread. He sullied a relationship crucial to the success of the prequels. He tainted the well water and primed himself for a battle that he could not win, would not win.

In 2004, clearly fatigued by criticism, Lucas responded to the outcry of fans who lamented the alterations to the original films: "I'm sorry that you saw a half-completed film and fell in love with it. But I want it to be the way I want it to be . . . I'm the one who has to have everybody throw rocks at me all the time, so at least if they're going to throw rocks at me, they're going to throw rocks at me for something I love rather than something I think is not very good."[10] His comment not only undermined a product beloved to fans but also ridiculed them for adoring something that he felt was only second-rate. This was a slap in the face of fans who loved the original films. Lucas seemed to be taking back his movies, taking them back from the fans, and bullying them for liking them in the first place—discounting what they loved and, in effect, discounting them.

There were fewer changes to *The Empire Strikes Back*, suggesting that Lucas agreed that it was a superior film to *A New Hope*. Perhaps Lucas felt a little gun-shy due to the initial outcry. There were more changes to *Return of the Jedi*, in particular to Jabba the Hut's palace band and the celebration at the end of the movie. The special edition sales for *Episode IV: A New Hope* propelled it past *ET* as the most lucrative film ever made, which may have been another reason why Lucas insisted that there be only one definitive edition of the film. Had there been more than one, the sales would have been split, and he would not have been able to boast creating the most profitable film of all time and beating out his friend and rival Steven Spielberg.

It took more than twenty drafts before Lucas was finally ready to show anyone the script for *Episode I*, which he called *The Beginning*. Nevertheless, on January 13, 1995, he felt confident enough to say that he had completed a rough draft. By early 1996 his art department was creating storyboards for an unfinished script. Lucas seemed to think that digital technology would make up for whatever the story lacked quickly and cheaply. Consequently, he had to revise the script during filming as well as in postproduction.

Despite filming every *Star Wars* movie since 1976 at Elstree Studios in London, Lucas passed on the sentimental choice and instead opted for a former Rolls-Royce factory ten miles away that had recently been converted to a movie studio for the James Bond movie *Goldeneye*. In the intervening years since *Return of the Jedi*, Lucas's tastes had clearly gotten a little more hoity-toity, and the former Rolls-Royce factory matched them more than the former Elstree site where, in the 1970s, the British crew terrorized him and called his Wookie a dog.

Once Lucas began making *Episode I*, he was for once actually enjoying himself, largely because he was excited about what he felt were the unlimited possibilities of digital filmmaking. When Lucas began casting for *Star Wars* in the early to mid-seventies, he was adamant about not wanting any famous actors. He almost did not cast Harrison Ford because he did not want any actors from his previous films, and Ford had already been in *American Graffiti*. This was not the case for *Episode 1*. His casting director, Robin Gurland, handled most of the casting duties over the course of two years and, despite not possessing a complete script, found proven actors all too willing to sign on to the next *Star Wars* movie. This was the case with Samuel L. Jackson, who made several public appeals to Lucas for any role no matter how small, even the role of an anonymous Stormtrooper. Liam Neeson was another famous actor who Gurland brought in. He had recently entered the realm of the A-list on the wings of *Schindler's List*, directed by Lucas's buddy Steven Spielberg. Lucas loved the idea of casting Neeson and felt he would bring to the role something similar to what Alec Guinness brought to the first *Star Wars*.

Principal photography for *Episode I* began on June 26, 1997. Lucas's title for the film was still *The Beginning*, and security was tight. All cast and crew were required to wear nametags. Lucas's nametag said Yoda. Not much had changed in relation to how Lucas treated actors. He did not care in the least that, for this film, he was using veteran actors who already made their bones and won high honors such as Academy Awards. He was still not interested in method acting drills or any such nonsense. To Lucas's major disappointment, digital technology had actually not advanced to the point where he could shoot the entire film digitally. Nevertheless, he pressed on, shooting what scenes he could digitally and then converting these to film for theaters. Principal photography wrapped on September 30, 1997.

In November 1998, Lucas released the first footage of *The Phantom Menace* via trailer. Theaters reported that fans came to the films where the trailer was showing, but nearly half of them left before the feature film started. The following year, fans began camping out six weeks ahead of the release in order to be among the first to see the film. This was another indication that fans were willing to go through just about anything to see the film, to prove their fandom. The notion of camping outside of a movie theater was totally irrational behavior. It was not as though the fans were in jeopardy of not seeing the film. The film was not like a live concert that only happens once in real time. The exact same film would be played over and over again as long as there were fans willing to pay the price of admission. So why did fans subject themselves to the discomfort of the elements to see the film? It belies rationality but seems appropriate in the world of *Star Wars* fandom.

Several teams from various websites and fan groups united and camped out in shifts outside San Francisco's Coronet Theatre. One man, Shanti Seigel, claimed his reason for camping out was that he wanted to sit in a particular seat for the first showing. Fans endured bad weather and an onslaught of drive-by insults, including being pummeled by water balloons filled with maple syrup, all to be one of the first fans to see *Star Wars*. There had to be some built-up resentment just under the surface. All the pain and suffering was worth it as long as the film delivered. If the film was amazing, it would be worth it. No one could imagine the film not being great. Their reference points were not only the original films, even the doctored original films, but also the extended universe inside their minds, a universe they had created through the toys and other artifacts that facilitated a certain amount of fan ownership. How could the films not be great?

A week before the midnight show, George Lucas showed up outside the Coronet Theatre to visit with the campers and shake hands. He was offering a sneak preview to Hollywood royalty that night at the Coronet. This was a little strange optically. Lucas invited celebrities like Robin Williams to the screening while the fans who had been camping out for three weeks looked on wistfully. When a Lucasfilm rep surreptitiously told a few of the campers that there were a couple seats left, the group made a decision that no one would break ranks and see the film ahead of time. They had created a family, and it was important to them to maintain solidarity in the face of temptation. However, a few did take the opportunity to join the dark side next to Lucas at his throne. That night, fans saw Coppola smoking a cigar for half an hour and were aghast that he was missing a chunk of the film for a cigar break. When asked, he told them that he had seen bits of it before. Perhaps this should have been an indication of the film's excitement level.[11]

When the big day finally arrived on May 19, 1999, at least one camper, who encountered reporters right after the film, was not impressed: "Shit. Fucking. Sandwich"[12] was his assessment, before sauntering off into the night, presumably to his own bed.

During the 1990s, Lucasfilm left most fanzines alone as they migrated to the internet, provided that the material did not stray from what had been codified in their letter decades before, resulting in a sort of self-regulation among fanzine publishers. One 1996 letter from Lucasfilm noted,

> Lucasfilm appreciates *Star Wars* fans' support and we want you to be able to communicate with one another. Your energy and enthusiasm makes you an important part of our *Star Wars* family. As you can understand, it is important, as well, for Lucasfilm to protect the *Star Wars* copyrights and trademarks. Since the internet is growing so fast, we are in the process of developing guidelines for how we can enhance the ability of *Star Wars* fans to communicate with each other without infringing on *Star Wars* copyrights and trademarks and we hope to make these

guidelines available in the near future. As we prepare for the *Star Wars* Trilogy Special Edition which will be coming to theatres next year and as we begin pre-production on the upcoming "prequels," we are now entering an exciting new *Star Wars* era. Many thanks for your support and interest.[13]

It was clear that Lucasfilm was very much aware of *Star Wars* activity on the internet, especially fanfic. In 1997, Marc Hedlund, director of Lucasfilm's internet development, reconfirmed the 1981 policy that "the company tolerates the publication of fan fiction, so long as the stories are not for commercial gain and don't sully the family image of the *Star Wars* characters."[14] Nevertheless, around this time there were a flurry of cease-and-desist letters issued by Lucasfilm's attorneys with the goal of shutting down some *Star Wars*–related websites and preventing the circulation of fan fiction. In general, *Star Wars* was the most aggressive franchise fans had ever seen when it came to controlling and silencing fan cultural production.

Lucasfilm never made its policy exactly clear. No one really knew what the company considered "sullying." The corporation ruled by threats and intimidation, the same sort of bullying that Lucas experienced as a child. Now that he was a corporate hotshot with his own castle and fawning subjects, he could bully the nerds with impunity, especially those nerds who enjoyed casting his characters in homosexual roles.

Lucasfilm's attitude toward fan film was a lot more lenient than it was with fanfic. Fans were welcome to create their films as long as they did not profit from them. As long as no original actors appeared in the films, and fan filmmakers used no footage from the originals, fans were welcome to create *Star Wars* fan films. Lucas appreciated young filmmakers showing him respect by making films within the *Star Wars* universe. Conversely, Lucas had no patience for writers who attempted to expand his vision, especially in relation to sexuality and gender. Lucas's insecurity as a writer informed his privileging of film. Ever since his days at USC, Lucas considered himself a poor writer. This fact, coupled with his discomfort when it came to sex, positioned fan writers on extremely shaky ground.

In the spring of 1998, *Entertainment Weekly* profiled digital filmmaker Kevin Rubio. His ten-minute short film *Troops* (1998) drew the interest of several Hollywood studios, several of whom offered him financing for his next project. *Troops* focuses on a group of Stormtroopers whose job it is to police Tatooine. Lucas was so impressed with the film that he gave Rubio a job writing for *Star Wars* comics. Fans were aware that Lucas paid attention to their work, especially their films. Lucasfilm even held a fan film contest called the *Star Wars* Fan

Cinema Competition, and George Lucas selected the winner. These acts were not very consistent with Lucasfilm's history of trying to control fan culture.

Lucasfilm did in fact draw a line with fan films. When one fan film called *The Dark Redemption* (1999) by Peter Mether incorporated brief clips from *Return of the Jedi* and featured actor Peter Sumner, who appeared in *A New Hope*, Lucasfilm fired off a cease-and-desist letter to the filmmakers and shut down the website. The film was made for an Australian film competition and screened once in the United States before Lucasfilm stepped in.

Even so, there was a clear double standard when it came to fan films compared to fan fiction. Lucas was far less willing to tolerate fan fiction because there was a greater chance that these writers would take liberties with the characters.

Fan art was inherently good for business, as it demonstrated an engagement in the product that resulted in consumption and profit for the creator. Fans who create fan art are sometimes referred to as cultural poachers, but cultural producers are able to exploit the poachers for their production and free advertising in exchange for working within a copyrighted universe.[15]

The advent of the internet made fan culture more visible, providing a powerful new distribution channel for amateur cultural production that had hitherto been underground. When Amazon released the fan film *George Lucas in Love* (1999), it outsold *The Phantom Menace* in the first week. Many fan filmmakers viewed their foray into fan films as a way to break into the industry.

Just as the wave effect carried *Episode IV*, as word-of-mouth spread among kids all over the United States, a wave effect occurred right away with regard to *The Phantom Menace*. It became trendy to criticize the film and lay into George Lucas as a soulless dweeb, something he had worked his whole life to avoid. Along with black civil rights groups criticizing Lucas for the character of Jar Jar, homosexual groups accused Lucas of caricaturing a gay man. For those who went to the film in order to recapture that feeling they experienced when they were young, the movie was a bitter disappointment.

Lucas banked a lot of money before fans even saw the film. Hasbro paid him $400 million for the rights to the toys. LEGO joined in and entered into its first licensing agreement in the history of the Danish franchise. The *Star Wars* fan club reached its peak around the time of the release of *The Phantom Menace*, mailing out 2 million copies of *Star Wars* insider each month. Just as they did with the original films, many fans saw *The Phantom Menace* multiple times, if only to grasp their confusing reaction.

Fans were gobsmacked and thunderstruck that they did not love the film and returned, paying full price, again and again, to figure out exactly why they did not love it, why it fell short of the films of their youth, why they left the theater unsatisfied. Younger fans, however, loved the film, as they were unsaddled by the impossible expectations of adult fans, largely of their own making.

It was not long before the negative reviews started to pour in from some of the biggest news outlets in the country. *Time* and *Newsweek* panned the film. Peter Travers of *Rolling Stone* said, "The actors are wallpaper, the jokes are juvenile, there's no romance, and the dialogue lands with the thud of a computer-instruction manual." The *Washington Post* described the film as "Joyless, overly reverential and impenetrably plotted."[16] Even Roger Ebert's positive review admonished fans to ignore the bad dialogue and focus on all the goodies they can look at. Gallup took three polls in 1999, and each time the responses describing the film as excellent dropped, but the percentage of people assessing the film as poor never rose above 6 percent. In the final poll, 33 percent of people described it as excellent.

The film still made a boatload of money. In the first week, the film made $134 million. National Public Radio film critic Elvis Mitchell declared the film "critic-proof."[17] Nobody seemed to care that no one actually liked it. In fact, the bad reviews were part of the scene. Folks went to see it anyway.

The criticisms cut to the heart of Lucas. Reviewers attacked his tender spots, such as his insecurities as a writer and his awkward treatment of romance. They also undermined his strengths, such as the technical aspects of the film. *The Phantom Menace* was the most lucrative *Star Wars* film ever made, yet there was nowhere for Lucas to run.

Jake Lloyd more closely resembled a typical dweeb than the most powerful Sith Lord in the galaxy. By all accounts, fans were not impressed with his portrayal of the Dark Lord of the Sith as a young man at all. Whether he was too young, too cute, or simply the speaker of bad dialogue, the responses to the performance of a young Darth Vader were merciless and never-ending, so much so that Jake Lloyd quit acting after his role in *The Phantom Menace*. To make matters worse, the young actor's classmates brutally teased him in high school and college, and he eventually wound up in prison and diagnosed with schizophrenia. Bryan Young, a devout *Star Wars* blogger, once met Jake Lloyd at a party. Young, a stolid defender of *The Phantom Menace*, drunkenly cornered Lloyd and made his argument in defense of the film. Lloyd, then in his twenties, expressed his loathing for the franchise and shared his nightmare of being terrorized and bullied in high school and college for his performance. Young told Lloyd that he named his son Anakin. The former actor responded by extricating himself from the conversation and later unfriending Young on Facebook.[18]

Lloyd's experience could not have been more different from members of the original cast of the first *Star Wars* film, who were immediately deified and could not go out in public without being mobbed by adoring fans.

Negative fan reaction to *The Phantom Menace* also made some fans re-evaluate Lucas's role in the original films such as *The Empire Strikes Back*. Some fans began wondering whether the greatness of those films was really more attributable to director Irvin Kirshner, producer Gary Kurtz, or the two scriptwriters, Leigh Brackett and Lawrence Kasdan. In general, fans now viewed the untouchable George Lucas as fallible, if not a complete fraud. Even those folks who later claimed to enjoy *The Phantom Menace* only did so with the caveat that they were able to tune out Jar Jar.

Lucas dismissed fan disappointment as a generational divide and began writing *Episode II* in September 1999, only around four months after *Episode I* was released. He conceded that he had created a monster in his fan base and that there was no way he could satiate them. He believed that the younger generation did not feel the same way. He revisited the same arguments that he made for *Return of the Jedi*, claiming that the films were for kids, not the adults who had once been kids. This argument seemed disingenuous and like a cop-out to many fans. Why not try to please both his older fans and younger fans? Was it even possible? Had he created an insatiable monster? The response to *The Phantom Menace* knocked Lucas down a peg, despite transforming him from a millionaire to a billionaire. His legacy was sullied. When the chips were down and he had everything he could ever ask for—as far as resources and technology—for not one but three films, he dropped the ball.

Among the myriad ways Lucas dropped the ball, according to millions of fans, was the midichlorians. In the world of Star Wars, midichlorians were microscopic life-forms that functioned as conductors of the force. Some folks simply had more than others, better enabling them to access the force. Lucas felt there needed to be a stronger reason for Qui-Gon and Obi-Wan to begin training a ten-year-old boy in the ways of the force, and midichlorians provided a concrete reason why the two Jedi knights risked falling out of favor with the Jedi Council to train Anakin. They tested Anakin's blood for a particular ingredient that predisposed him to the force. According to Qui-Gon and Obi-Wan, Anakin's midichlorian levels were off the charts, in a territory never before seen, even greater than Yoda's levels, which also suggested that he could be the chosen one to bring balance to the force. The implication was that the midichlorians themselves might have birthed Anakin, that Anakin could have been a product of a virgin birth, a birth without sex. After all that had been surmised about Lucas, this detail seemed to be strangely in line with Lucas's values. Life without sex for Lucas would have been preferable.

One can understand why fans blanched at this development; it stifled the imagination. Midichlorians seemed to be on par with biological privilege rather than merit-based success. This fatalistic ingredient was far from the original notion that anyone could be a Jedi, which was more appealing to the fan base, not unlike the American dream. Because midichlorians were responsible for the power of the force, the force was undemocratic. The playing field was not equal. Not everyone could be a Jedi.

It was clear that the criticisms of Jar Jar Binks affected how Lucas employed the character in *Episodes II* and *III*, where his role shrank to nearly nonexistent. Further, Lucas never mentioned the midichlorians again in an episodic feature film, although they would appear again in the television show *The Clone Wars*. Lucas later admitted that the criticisms were wounding: "Oh it hurts. It hurts a great deal. But part of making movies is you get attacked, and sometimes in very personal ways."[19]

The general excuse for Lucas and for many at Lucasfilm was that nothing could have met the expectations of older fans, that older fans simply asked too much of Lucas in wanting him to re-create the excitement they experienced when they were young. This was perhaps true. Fan reaction to *The Phantom Menace* set a trend in the *Star Wars* franchise where it seemed as though real fans hated every *Star Wars* film since *Return of the Jedi*, including *Return of the Jedi*. *Star Wars* fans became some of the bitterest fans of any film franchise, ever. *Star Wars* fans hated *Star Wars*, and the more one hated the films, the more authentic the fan. Lucas was not ready for this kind of backlash, especially since the advent of the internet made all these fan opinions instantly public. There were fan websites devoted solely to hatred of Jar Jar Binks. Fan backlash to *The Phantom Menace* was a byproduct of all the success Lucas had up to that point. He set the table for fans to explode on him when he arrogantly changed the original films.

With *The Phantom Menace*, Lucas finally created a film exactly as he wanted it. The backlash was payback. The vitriol was out there. The internet removed the guesswork in terms of how fans felt. Even though Lucas said at times that he was not bothered by fan criticisms, he clearly was, noting, "I'm sorry if they don't like it. . . . They should go back and see *The Matrix* or something."[20]

Lucas was so upset by all the blowback that he refused to do any more promotional appearances, announcing that "I want people to like what I do. Everybody wants to be accepted at least by somebody. . . . But we live in a world now where you're forced to become part of this larger corporate entity called the media . . . I'd just as soon let my own films die than have to go out and sell them on a circuit. And I do as little as I have to, to feel responsible."[21] These were strange comments coming from a man who took over half a billion dollars from a toy manufacturer for the rights to the prequels. Lucas had already sold market saturation. It was too late to back out now simply because fans were not fawning over him and calling him a superior life form.

By the time Lucas released *The Phantom Menace* in theaters, he had already been writing *Episode II* for nearly a year. *Episode II* was the hardest *Star Wars* film to write, since much of it involved a love story and heavy dialogue, both of which were a struggle for Lucas. Lucas titled the draft *Jar Jar's Great Adventure*, once again finding it humorous to needle the fans.

Even amid the criticism, Lucas never stopped innovating technologically. He announced that for the first time in film history, he would shoot the second film completely digitally, which necessitated that theaters change their sound systems. More than once, Lucas changed the way movies sounded in theaters across America. Initially, he pressured theaters into converting their systems to Dolby Stereo, since he felt that in Dolby, *Star Wars* sounded like it did when he was mixing it. Then in the late 1980s, he started a wave that resulted in thousands of theaters switching to the THX sound system that his team created, its name a nod to his first film. Then in the 2000s, he pressured theaters all over the world to change their sound systems to accommodate digital films.

Casting for *Episode II* began in November 1999. Once again, Lucas forced casting director Robin Gurland to search for actors based on skeletal characters. Shooting was scheduled to start in May 2000, and Lucas was feeling the pressure at the end of 1999. Once April approached, Lucas gave up and hired screenwriter Jonathan Hales to come in and finish the script. Hales delivered his script on June 23, just before Lucas left for Sydney, Australia to begin shooting.

Perhaps the biggest bullying move that Lucasfilm came up with was in 2000 when the company decided to offer fans their own webspace on which to produce and distribute fan production. *Starwars.com* offered fans sixteen megabytes with which to play. Section 8.6 of the fan.starwars.com terms of service stated that "you hereby grant to us the right to exercise all intellectual property rights, in any media now known or not currently known, with respect to any content you place on your Homestead-powered website."[22] In short, Lucasfilm would have absolute control of any content created on the site, power to profit from it, and power to destroy it. Here was Lucas absolutely taking over the means of production and creating a space of exploitation and tyranny that dwarfed what Lucas rebelled against as a young filmmaker.

Fanfic authors such as Elizabeth Durack realized right away that this was not a magnanimous move on the part of George Lucas and Lucasfilm, but rather a strategic power move to remove any gray area as to the status of fan production, since Lucasfilm's clear ownership of the site and all the production on it was rock solid. Fanfic writers realized that the optics of Lucasfilm firing off cease-and-desist letters and shutting down websites damaged a brand that relied on its fandom for survival. The creation of the webspace allowed Lucasfilm to have total control without all the legal wrangling. The company could shut down fan production quietly and efficiently without having to explain itself at all.

In November 2000, Lucasfilm created the commercial digital cinema site Atomfilms.com as the official host for *Star Wars* fan films. The site provided a library of official sound effects and ran periodic contests to recognize outstanding amateur accomplishments. In return, participating filmmakers agreed to certain constraints on content. For example, films could only parody existing *Star Wars* films, rather than expand on them. No film could use extant *Star Wars* footage, but could use action figures as well as sanctioned clips from the available filmmaking kits provided by the site.

Media executive Chris Albrecht pointed out that Lucas was at risk of being sued for plagiarism if he viewed fan-produced material and then inadvertently created something similar down the road. Further, Albrecht noted that the quality of the fan art was so good that consumers did not know whether something was canon or not.[23] Lucasfilm had very little power to control parody or documentaries, as these enjoyed broad protections under current case law, but the company tolerated what it legally had to accept in return for being able to shut down what it might otherwise be unable to control.

Lucas began principal photography for *Episode II* on Monday, June 26, 2000. One of the first scenes that he shot was of actor Ian McDiarmid as Chancellor Palpatine at a podium in an elevated pod. The rest of the stage was blue screen. McDiarmid and the other actors found the lack of a traditional set unnerving. Lucas was interested in creating all his sets digitally, despite the discomfort of his actors. Morale increased when a very real R2D2 showed up on set. Several members of the ILM staff groused that there was no real artistry in digital moviemaking, that it was mostly just a technical process. Lucas, of course, did not care what they thought and continued unabashedly. For Lucas, much of life was a technical process. Lucas wrapped up physical photography on September 20.

By the time Lucas released the title of the second film, *Attack of the Clones*, fans groaned and laughed at him. Lucas defended the title and said it was an homage to the serials that had inspired *Star Wars* to begin with. Even so, fans had already dug in and were ready to pants the director and throw his shoes into the neighboring lawn. Worse, they were ready to pay back some of the bullying that Lucas had gotten away with over the years. Lucas decided to scale back the merchandising for *Episode II*, admitting that they had probably gone overboard with the first film. Lucas's decision to limit the merchandising back in the 1970s to quality products was seemingly out the window with the prequels, evidenced by Qui-Gon Jinn neckties.

In a move that was perhaps too little, too late, Lucas made a huge concession to a group of webmasters who oversaw *Star Wars* websites. He invited them to Skywalker Ranch and handed out autographed copies of the *Episode I* DVD. He also answered questions for twenty minutes. This was a capitulation to the beating Lucas was taking online, and the way he handled it indicated that he felt the criticisms were personal, as though, if he just befriended his critics or invited the bullies to his haunted garage, they would like him and go easy on him. Lucas seemed to think that the criticisms directed at him were simply personal rather than aesthetic—and perhaps he was correct in that assumption—but by now it was out of the hands of the few and into the hands of the legion of fans disillusioned with their God and his films.

Another genre of fan fiction, dominated by women, was fan videos, which often spliced together extant footage from films or shows and highlighted or expanded on different aspects of the characters. Diane Williams's *Come What May* (2001) was a good example of a fan song-vid that explored the relationship between Obi-Wan and Qui-Gon from *The Phantom Menace*, a relationship that dominated post-prequel *Star Wars* slash fiction, to Lucas's utter horror.[24] A typical song-vid used images from an existing film to explore the relationships between its characters in a different way. This video focused on and repeated images of Obi-Wan Kenobi holding Qui-Gon Jinn after Jinn is killed by Darth Maul. The images unfold as the song "Come What May," from the soundtrack of Baz Luhrmann's *Moulin Rouge!* (2001), plays. Many fans read *Come What May* as slash.

Perhaps the greatest testament to the global impact that *Star Wars* had on a generation was the emergence of Jediism as a religion. Joke or not, this happening pointed to the religious experience of a generation who, through the films and the toys, experienced a taste of what it meant to create. In February 2001, New Zealanders were one week away from filling out their once-a-decade census. An anonymous New Zealander, still unidentified to this day, sent out an email blast encouraging folks to check "other" for question 18 that asked one to designate his or her religion. The email encouraged folks to write in "Jedi" as their preferred religion. The goal was to get Jediism recognized as a state-recognized religion. The amazing result was that 53,715 New Zealanders wrote in Jediism as their religion. Even though the government ultimately refused to acknowledge it as such, Jediism unofficially became the second most popular religion in New Zealand.[25]

A similar email was sent out in Australia, where the government allowed that if 10,000 people wrote in Jedi, then Jediism would become an official religion. The email noted that by writing in Jedi, one would automatically be a Jedi knight. The Australian government responded by warning that anyone who intentionally falsified any census data would be subject to a $1,000 fine. The government also stipulated that for a religion to be included in the Australian Bureau of Statistics, the group would have to demonstrate a foundational belief system for the religion in question. Over 70,000 Australians outed themselves as Jedi. No one was fined.

Jediism caught on fast, as similar occurrences happened in Vancouver, Croatia, the Czech Republic, and Montenegro. Officials in these countries realized there were thousands of Jedi citizens. The United Kingdom had the largest population of Jedi with over 400,000, making it the fourth-largest religion in Britain behind Christianity, Islam, and Hinduism. The deep and lasting impact of the films on a generation had effects that manifested in strange ways, like a half a million people around the world claiming it as their religion. It is not surprising that Lucas wound up in conflict with some of his acolytes whose lives were fundamentally changed by the films and the toys. As fans, they made sense of their world through the prism of the *Star Wars* universe.

Jim Ward, vice president of marketing for Lucasfilm, told *New York Times* reporter Amy Harmon in 2002: "We've been very clear all along on where we draw the line. We love our fans. We want them to have fun. But if in fact somebody is using our characters to create a story unto itself, that's not in the spirit of what we think fandom is about. Fandom is about celebrating the story the way it is."[26] Lucasfilm, and George Lucas in particular, were very inconsistent when it came to how they responded to fan cultural production. On one hand, Lucas clearly liked the attention and respect inherent in pastiche and even parody. On the other hand, Lucas and Lucasfilm never completely allowed fans to operate with total freedom.

Jeanne Cole, a spokesperson for Lucasfilm, remarked, "What can you do? How can you control it? As we look at it, we appreciate the fans, and what would we do without them? If we anger them, what's the point?"[27] For some fan fiction writers, their fan work functioned as a ticket into the world of publishing. Lucas's offer of free webspace, however, precluded fans from owning the rights to their work without compensation of any kind. There was a certain genius in Lucasfilm offering fans webspace that positioned the company as both generous and more controlling than ever.[28] *Star Wars* had become a sort of cultural mythology, not unlike the gods of Greek and Roman myth or the lore of Native Americans. It was very hard for Lucasfilm to control a mythology, and questionable as to whether it still had a right to.

While there was no clear policy from Lucasfilm, *Star Wars* fan fiction became ubiquitous all over the web. Webmasters on these sites claimed to deal with Lucasfilm all the time on a whole range of matters. Fan fiction writers remained apprehensive about the knowledge that Lucasfilm had the legal right to remove any content it wished.

Once *Attack of the Clones* was released on May 16, 2002, in 3,161 theaters, fans attacked, making fun of the dialogue and especially the romance between Anakin and Padme, which most found over-the-top and cheesy. Lucas doubled down and argued that anything that anyone did not like was on purpose and was not a flaw in the film. Lucas appeared to be losing all sense of himself as an artist in terms of taking criticism.

*Los Angeles Times* critic Patrick Goldstein, in an article called "Seclusion Has Left Lucas Out of Touch," proffered that there was no one left on Lucas's team to give him an honest assessment of the work, that he had created a company full of yes people. Goldstein wrote, "No one seems to deliver bad news . . . Lucas's best work was made with strong collaborators. . . . [His] talents are probably better suited as a conceptual thinker and producer than director."[29] Lucas responded by irrationally using the comments as an indictment of derailed democracy due to individual squeaky wheels: "That's one of the problems of a democracy. You get these individual voices that are very loud, and very dysfunctional. . . . And if you cater to those voices, you end up with a very dysfunctional society."[30] These comments were in stark contrast to comments that Lucas made back in the 1970s about wresting the means of production from the studios and delivering them into the hands of the people. Lucas was now part of the movie-making bourgeoisie.

*Star Wars* fans who loathed the first two episodes had their personal ways of coping with the films. Some re-edited the films themselves; some turned to fan fiction in order to explore minor characters; and some simply watched the films over and over in a Freudian death drive, returning to the scene of the trauma and trying to change it or correct it, hoping it came out differently—a form of insanity.

Discussions of the merits of the first two prequels once again largely centered on generational gulfs, the idea that adult fans expected too much from the prequels, expected that they would be moved as they were moved when they were in grade school. Others faulted the overreliance on CGI at the expense of character. There was a certain paradox in fan ire for Lucas. On one hand, many fans owed a large chunk of their identity to Lucas for his creation, but on the other hand, fans felt as though Lucas owed them for their decades of devotion. Lucas was responsible for carrying the torch of a cultural myth that had grown larger than he had. He was the steward of people's childhoods.

Many remarked that there was very little tension in the movies, that they were more about the special effects. The characters lacked emotion, and there was very little banter in the films. In the originals, Han's cockiness and sarcasm played well against the seriousness of Obi-Wan and the greenness of Luke. According to fans, there was none of that in the prequels.

Many suggested the slide already began to take shape with *Return of the Jedi* and the introduction of the Ewoks, or "care bears," as some derisively referred to the creatures from Endor. Others cited the alterations of the original trilogy as the point at which they lost all faith in Lucas. One fan noted, "the rot set in when the original trilogy was re-raked during the Special Editions and you find out that all the things you loved about the original films were other people's ideas, and were things that GL might have vetoed if he'd had the chance."[31]

Amid the ever-growing negative sentiments surrounding the prequels, Lucas pressed on. He knew that the third and final film would make or break all three films. Most of what he envisioned for the backstory would happen in the third film. His primary goals were to dramatize Anakin's turn to the dark side as well as connect the prequels seamlessly to the original trilogy, no small feat on both counts.

It took Lucas a long time to begin writing *Episode III*, but by mid-December 2002, he was once again at his desk four days a week, channeling his youth. He continued writing through the holidays on his yellow legal pad. He quickly came up with the title, *Revenge of the Sith*, a nod to the abandoned title of his third *Star Wars* film, *Revenge of the Jedi*. Lucas completed the draft on January 31, 2003, and began filming four days later until he wrapped in mid-September.

For *Episode III*, Lucas knew what he had to do. This would be where Anakin finally gives in to the dark side. This would be the first *Star Wars* film to earn a PG-13 rating because of the violence, violence that had been alluded to since the beginning. Still, Lucas tempered his expectations: "It's not a happy movie by any stretch of the imagination. . . . It's a tragedy. . . . It will probably be the least successful of all the *Star Wars* movies—but I know that."[32]

Lucas was wrong once again. *Revenge of the Sith* premiered on May 19, 2005, and set a single-day box office record of $50 million with an opening weekend take of $108 million and $848 million worldwide. Critics changed their tune. Writers from the *New York Times*, *Variety*, and *Newsweek*, who had panned the first two episodes, applauded Lucas for returning to form. Despite the success of *Episode III*, Lucas was weary. He appeared on *60 Minutes* in 2005 and was asked about his love life, to which he responded, "What love life?"[33]

In 2008, filmmaker Kevin Smith released *Zack and Miri Make a Porno*, which plays upon and exploits the restrained sexuality just under the surface of the *Star Wars* franchise.[34] Desperate financial straits compel two friends, Zack and Miri, to make a porno, especially after Miri becomes an internet sensation after two customers post a film of her wearing granny panties and changing into her uniform at a coffee shop where she is employed. From then on, she is known all over the internet as Granny Panties.

Zack and Miri decide to call their film *Star Whores* in order to target comic book and science fiction nerds. The film's characters include Princess Layher, Lube Skyballer, Hung Solo, On-your-knees Bend-over, ICUP, R2TBag, and Darth Vibrator. Zack notes that the film will be an erotic reimagining or parody of the classic film. In their reimagining, Darth Vibrator is a bad girl who wants to fuck the galaxy. Lube and Hung must stop her. The spoof never happens because the city condemns and demolishes their studio, but the idea draws attention to the sexual possibilities of *Star Wars*, on which slash writers often capitalize.

Once the dust settled on the prequels, it became clear to Lucas that he was most successful when he collaborated as part of a creative team. Lucas also remembered that the idea for *Star Wars* began with the *Flash Gordon* television serials, and that his first love was animation. When USC awarded him the Samuel Warner Memorial Scholarship in 1968 and the opportunity to work at the Warner Bros. studio for six months in any department with a stipend of $80 a week, his first choice was the animation department, but it was mostly dormant. With a *Star Wars* animated television show, Lucas would not have to deal with actors. By 2000, computer animation had progressed to the point where Lucas felt he could pull off a first-rate animated TV series. Lucas had not given up on the prequels and realized that much of the story of the collapse of the Republic and the destruction of the Jedi took place off-screen. There was still so much opportunity for stories taking place during the Clone Wars.

In addition to *The Clone Wars* animated series, Lucas was deeply involved in making a live-action television series called *Star Wars Underworld*. Both ABC and HBO were interested in the live-action show that centered on the former Republic capital Coruscant in the two decades between *Revenge of the Sith* and *A New Hope*. The show would focus on the shadier characters in the universe, such as the bounty hunters, gangsters, and pirates. Boba Fett was rumored to be a recurring character. The show would harken back to the franchise's space-western, steam-punk roots. Rick McCallum, the show's co-executive producer along with Lucas, envisioned a cost-effective, largely interior drama, while Lucas envisioned lots of expensive speeder bike chases and pod-style drag races. One heated argument between the two coproducers centered on the character Jar Jar Binks. Lucas mentioned including the character in the show, and McCallum hit the roof.[35] One needed to be firm with Lucas when it came to Jar Jar. Jar Jar was a misfit, a pariah, a nerd, who bumbled his way to amazing success. Jar Jar Binks was Lucas.

The price tag for each episode of *Underworld* was estimated to be $11 million—just too expensive with the available technology. Lucas shelved the show, but it would later re-emerge under Disney Lucasfilm as *The Mandalorian*.

*The Clone Wars* began as a series of short cartoons in 2002, created by Russian animator Genndy Tartakovsky for Cartoon Network in order to get fans excited for *Episode III*. While Lucas liked Tartakovsky's work, for which he won an Emmy, Lucas felt he could do better. With a deal in place with Cartoon Network, Lucas's goal was to make at least one hundred episodes. All he needed was a creative director that he could trust. Everyone knew that Dave Filoni, a writer for the animated show *Avatar: The Last Airbender* as well as an animator on *King of the Hill*, was a huge *Star Wars* fan. He dressed up as Jedi Master Plo Koon for the premier of *Revenge of the Sith*. When a Lucas assistant called Filoni to invite him to Skywalker Ranch, Filoni thought it was a practical joke. It was not.

Filoni's initial idea was to focus the show on a team of Jedi and smugglers investigating the black market. Anakin and Obi-Wan would be characters in the main show but not the focus. Filoni came up with five new characters and presented them to Lucas at their meeting. Lucas shot down the idea, saying that he was happy with his characters. However, he did like one of Filoni's characters, Asla, for Anakin's padawan.

Lucas's model for *The Clone Wars* was the 1960s British animated television series *The Thunderbirds*. He wanted the show to have a unique look, similar to the painted wooden puppets on *Thunderbirds*. Achieving this effect required a blending of 2-D and 3-D computer animation technology.

After a few years of production, Lucas made a snap decision to release the first four episodes as a movie. This was a bad idea. There were no licensing agreements or marketing of any kind in place. Lucasfilm announced the movie in February of 2008, and it premiered only six months later. The film was released by Warner Bros. Forty years after Lucas earned his Warner Bros. scholarship and wanted to work in the company's animation department, he released an animated movie with the studio. At ninety-eight minutes, *The Clone Wars* was the first *Star Wars* movie with a running time of less than two hours. It was also the first not scored by John Williams. The production cost, $8.5 million, was the official budget for the original *Star Wars*. Despite Pepsi having a ten-year licensing agreement with Lucasfilm, they were unaware that the movie was even coming out.

Critics hated it. *Entertainment Weekly* critic Owen Gleiberman wrote, "it's no longer escapism. . . . It's something you want to escape from" and called Lucas "the enemy of fun." Roger Ebert, a consummate George Lucas and *Star Wars* apologist, described the movie as "a deadening film that cuts corners on its animation and slumbers through a plot that a) makes us feel like we've seen it all before, and b) makes us wish we hadn't."[36]

James Arnold Taylor, who provided the voice for Obi-Wan, realized that the show was not ready for the big screen. "We were still working out the storytelling," he noted, "the look and feel of the characters. . . . I'm not knocking it—I just feel we could have had a better start."[37] Nevertheless, *The Clone Wars* made $68.2 million at the box office, roughly eight times its budget. Financially, it was more successful than *Revenge of the Sith* and *Attack of the Clones.*

When *The Clone Wars* premiered on Cartoon Network, it was the highest rated premier in Cartoon Network history. The series involved lots of characters, and the stories clumped together in story arcs. The episodes without commercials lasted about twenty minutes each, similar to the *Flash Gordon* serials.

Lucas mentored Filoni by encouraging him to draw his stories from old war movies. He even showed him the dogfight footage he used for *A New Hope*. Lucas hardly talked to the animators and artists, but he loved meeting with the writers once a week to share his ideas. Lucas conveyed his story and character ideas to a team of writers and then let them figure out exactly how to execute it. His creative method for *The Clone Wars* was similar to Stan Lee's creative process at Marvel in the 1960s, known as the Marvel method. Essentially, Lee related to the artists the characters the general story, including the beginning and ending and the primary conflict; then it was up to the artists to fill in the rest, including major plot points, after which Lee wrote the dialogue and exposition.

Lucas was especially helpful when it came to stories about the Clones themselves. He had established the origins of the Clones in *Episode II: Attack of the Clones* as a Sith plot to destroy the Jedi. The Clones were modeled after Jango Fett, played by Maori actor Temuera Morrison. In Lucas's hands, individual Clones developed unique personalities, and *The Clone Wars* television series followed a group of them, including Rex, Cody, and Fives. The Clones are the most tragic figures in the *Star Wars* universe, and their story arc in *The Clone Wars* is the best in the series.

*The Clone Wars* television show dramatized the tension within Lucas concerning humanity and technology, as represented by the Clone army and the droid army. He was clearly in favor of the human Clones but sometimes betrayed sympathy for the droids. One thematic undercurrent in the *Star Wars* universe that also permeated Lucas's early work was the perversion of the natural by the technological, as illustrated by Darth Vader.

Lucas always had a strange and complex relationship with machines and technology. He was drawn to them, whether it was to cars or to the technological aspects of filmmaking. He excelled most in the technical aspects of film-making and struggled as a writer and a storyteller. His early short films, such as *6-18-67*, *1:42.08*, and *Electronic Labyrinth THX 1138 4EB*, all dealt with the dehumanizing effects of technology. Even in *American Graffiti*, the cars themselves vie for supremacy over the human beings. The cars at times are more sensual than the women. The men in the film desire and fawn over the cars more than over the women. Relationships with women are dysfunctional. The cars are more reliable and just as beautiful. The film ends when a machine nearly kills one of the heroes.

Droids are the pariahs of the *Star Wars* universe. They are constantly sneered at, made fun of, and bullied. In *A New Hope*, R2D2 and C3PO are not allowed into the cantina bar. Droids in general are second-class citizens. However, they are also capable of heroism. Characters often warn each other never to underestimate a droid, in terms of their deadliness as well as their capacity for heroism.

*The Clone Wars* television series sets up a dichotomy between the Clones and the droids. There are weapons designed to kill all organic matter while leaving machines untouched, and weapons designed to do the opposite. In a season 5 story arc covering episodes 10–12, a group of droids called the D-Squad led by Artoo and a diminutive Jedi named Colonel Meebur Gascon find themselves stranded on a desolate planet described as the void. While the Colonel loses his mind in the void, the droids take over and carry the group to safety. One droid sacrifices himself for the benefit of others, proving himself capable of the highest form of selflessness. The droids encounter a Clone with amnesia named Gregor working as a dishwasher. When Gregor realizes who he is, he too sacrifices himself for the group, thus demonstrating that both droids and Clones are capable of self-sacrifice for the benefit of others.

The plight of the Clones involves their humanizing transition from life created in a lab to fully functioning and critical thinking human beings with individuality and free will. One big difference between the Republic and the Separatists is that the Republic and the Jedi value the lives of the Clones and their droids, while the Separatists care very little for their battle droids who try to overwhelm the opposition with their sheer numbers. The battle droids' constant chatter of "Roger Roger" indicates their lack of individuality, despite their often comic dialogue, such as when one claims to be capable of independent thought to which several reply, "Roger Roger."

In the second season's episode 10, "The Deserter," Commander Rex finds a Clone deserter who has settled down as a farmer to raise a family. The deserter helps Rex fend off an attack by Separatist battle droids and, as a result, decides not to turn him in. The desertion of the Clone Trooper indicates his ability for independent thought and suggests that not all Clones are cut out to be soldiers.

In the first episode of season 6, "The Unknown," Clone Trooper Tup unwittingly executes Jedi Master Tiplar, setting off a story that ends with the realization that Clones were preprogrammed from the very beginning on the world of Kamino with a chip that will eventually cause them to turn on the Jedi. Clone Trooper Fives finds out about the plot and removes his chip but perishes before he can tell the rest of the Clone Army and the Jedi what he has found. Order 66 nicely frames Lucas's feelings about technology. On one hand, technology can be a perverting force, but on the other hand, humans are also perfectly capable of betrayal.

Perhaps the best story arc in *The Clone Wars* occurs in season 4, episodes 7–10 and centers on the battle of Umbara, demonstrating the Clones' ability to think independently and the fraternal love they have for one another. When the Separatists tighten their grip over vital supply routes near the planet Umbara, the Republic sends Jedi Master Pong Krell, Jedi Knight Anakin Skywalker, and Obi-Wan Kenobi to retake Umbara. When Anakin is forced to temporarily turn over command of his Clone Troopers to a new commander, the Jedi Pong Krell, conflict ensues as Krell sends the Clones on a deadly mission to take the capital of Umbara.

Rex and Fives stand up to him, voicing their protests and pointing out that, while they are aware of the importance of their mission, they are concerned about the welfare of their men. Against Krell's orders, Clone Troopers Fives, Jesse, and Hardcase embark on a mission to destroy a key supply ship that would allow them to win the battle. During the mission, Hardcase sacrifices himself and destroys the supply ship. Upon return, Krell court-martials Jesse and Fives and sentences them to death. Krell orders a group of Clone Troopers to execute the disgraced Troopers, but they refuse. When the Clones find out Krell's intention to become a Sith apprentice, they arrest him. The Troopers realize that if Krell is set free, he will likely give away the Republic's security codes and other intelligence. Knowing that this cannot happen, Clone Trooper

Dogma executes him, illustrating that while the Clones are allies with the Jedi, they are not limited by the Jedi code forbidding them to execute a Jedi traitor.

Another recurrent theme in *The Clone Wars* revolves around global imperialism and colonial occupation. In several episodes, the Separatists take over whole planets, enslave the inhabitants, and plunder their resources. It is then up to the Clones and the Jedi to liberate these people. In the first season's episode 20, "Innocents of Ryloth," the Separatists and droid armies use the Ryloth people as human shields against the Jedi and the Clone army.

The series features many of the same idiosyncrasies of the *Star Wars* universe. For example, throughout the six seasons, there are many examples of aggressive genital monsters threatening the heroes at every turn. There are phallic eels, slugs, and monstrous gaping holes aching to swallow up whole worlds.

The Jedi code forbidding romantic attachments plays a large role in the series as well, as Padme and Anakin must hide their love for one another. Additionally, Obi-Wan must come to terms with the fact that being a Jedi prohibited him from the love of his life, the leader of Mandalore, Duchess Satine Kryze. Maul kills her by driving the Mandalorian darksaber into her stomach right in front of Obi-Wan; with her last dying breath, she pledges her love to him.

Anakin's possessiveness and jealousy come to a head in season 6, episode 6, "The Rise of Clovis," when Padme's former boyfriend, Rush Clovis, attempts to sell out the Republic by making a shady deal with the banking system. Anakin catches Clovis and Padme embracing and nearly kills Clovis and batters Padme. Anakin comes off as an out-of-control violent abuser in the episode, anticipating the violence he carries out against Padme in *Revenge of the Sith*.

The show initially targeted an older audience by airing on Friday nights at 9 p.m. and offering very dark episodes with more violence than *Star Wars* fans had ever seen. Over 3 million viewers tuned in for the first season. The audience dropped to 1.6 million for season 4. For season 5, Cartoon Network moved the show to Saturday mornings at 9:30 a.m., but the ratings did not change.

Lucas always claimed that he made *Star Wars* for kids, and this fact bore out when data showed that the number one demographic for *The Clone Wars* was boys ages nine to fourteen, which was and remains *Star Wars'* core demographic.

*The Clone Wars* is by far the darkest *Star Wars* offering among the films and television shows. Anakin's struggle to reign in his emotions at times causes him to force choke his adversaries. In season 2, episode 13, "Voyage of Temptation," Anakin brutally kills a Mandalorian leader after he threatens to detonate a bomb. In the hands of Filoni, General Grievous is a lunatic killer, scarier than Heath Ledger's Joker. Grievous routinely taunts and executes Jedi and other allies of the Republic. The series depicts many point-blank executions as well as suicides and beheadings. In one particularly unsettling scene in season 3, episode 2, the Sith apprentice to Count Dooku, Asajj Ventress, kisses a Clone as he falls to the ground just after skewering him with her lightsaber.

With *The Clone Wars*, Lucas was able to tell the full backstory of the rise and fall of Darth Vader, after which he was done. He had clearly had it with the fans, but upset them further when he made additional changes to the original trilogy for the Blu-ray release in 2011. Particularly upsetting to fans was Vader's anguished lament just before he pulls the Emperor off Luke and throws him over the railing to his death. For some, that was a sign that Lucas not only did not care about his fans but actually loathed them. Lucas would sell the franchise the following year.

Season 5 of *The Clone Wars* ended on March 2, 2013, with Ahsoka leaving the Jedi Order after being wrongly accused for bombing the Jedi temple. There were big plans for season 6. One of the Clones would discover the terrifying truth about Order 66, and Yoda would go on a galactic voyage that would allow him to commune with the dead and learn the secret of how to become a force ghost. However, George Lucas sold Lucasfilm to Disney, and Kathleen Kennedy was not nearly as enamored with the show as Lucas and Filoni. Lucasfilm Disney officially canceled *The Clone Wars* in 2013. The show's fans assumed that Disney did not want a show that aired on a rival subsidiary. Under Disney, however, *Star Wars* simply did not have the financial backing it once enjoyed. The budget of roughly $2 million per episode was simply not viable, given the ratings. In the end, the decision to cancel the series came down to money.

Kennedy retained animation supervisor Dave Filoni and his key talent. She arranged for the remaining *Clone Wars* episodes to be released on Netflix. *Star Wars Rebels*, Filoni's second animated TV series, arising from the ashes of *Clone Wars*, was supposed to be better and cheaper than its predecessor. Set fourteen years after the events of *Episode III* and five years before the events of the original *Star Wars* trilogy, *Star Wars Rebels* follows a motley group of anti-Imperial youths on the planet of Lothal, recently occupied by the Empire. Kanan Jarrus, voiced by Freddie Prinze Jr., plays a moody renegade Jedi who escaped the Order 66 massacre. The crew of his ship *Ghost* comprises Ezra, Zeb, Sabine, Hera, and a grumpy astromech droid named Chopper.

This was virgin territory in the *Star Wars* universe that Lucas had reserved for the prequels. In a nod to fans of the original trilogy, Filoni based all his concept art for *Rebels* on the paintings and sketches of Ralph McQuarrie. When Filoni revealed the first batch of concept art from *Rebels* at Celebration Europe in July 2013, he did so surrounded by 501st Legion members dressed not as traditional Stormtroopers but as the McQuarrie concept versions, armed with laser swords. Filoni offered, "Ralph's designs are as real a part of *Star Wars* as anything that existed on the screen."[38]

There are a number of interesting developments in the *Star Wars* universe that take place in *Rebels*. For example, Commander Rex joins the fight against the Empire and suggests that the Clones had a choice as to whether to follow Order 66 but overwhelmingly decided to follow orders, pointing to humanity's rare capacity for moral courage in the face of tyranny. In season 3, episode 6, Rex and the gang encounter a battalion of battle droids who avoided deactivation at the end of the Clone Wars. Both Rex and the battle droids are interested in resuming their fight, causing Ezra to realize their similarities. Ezra forges a short-term alliance between the two by pointing out that in the Clone Wars, neither side won and the true victor was the Empire. In the final story arc, Hera pledges her love to Kanan, marking the most authentic love story in the history of *Star Wars*, and intelligent space whales called Purgill, resembling space sperm, aid the rebels in defeating Grand Admiral Thrawn. The powerful love story and the beneficent space sperm both distinguish the show contradistinctively from a George Lucas–helmed franchise.

# 6

# THIS IS THE WAY

After George Lucas sold the *Star Wars* franchise to Disney in October 2012, the only individual shareholder who owned more of Disney than Lucas was Steven P. Jobs, largely from the sale of Pixar, which Lucas still referred to as his company. Not long after the official signing, Lucas made a formal statement to the press, expressing that it was time for him to pass *Star Wars* on to a new generation of filmmakers. He reassured the public that he was confident that under Kathleen Kennedy's leadership at Lucasfilm and the aegis of Disney, *Star Wars* would live on for generations to come.[1] Passing the *Star Wars* franchise on to a new generation of filmmakers under Disney's control would prove harder than anyone thought.

Kennedy almost immediately promised a new *Star Wars* movie by the fall of 2015. She quickly brought in J. J. Abrams to direct and Lawrence Kasdan to handle the screenwriting duties. Abrams was a significant choice, as he had rebooted the *Star Trek* franchise in 2013 when he directed *Star Trek: Into Darkness*, which some critics found grossly derivative of *Star Trek II: The Wrath of Khan*. The transition from *Star Trek* to *Star Wars* annoyed many *Star Trek* fans who found the jump to be an opportunistic betrayal of their beloved franchise. Lucas mentored Abrams just as he mentored Dave Filoni on *The Clone Wars*. Abrams was not another Richard Marquand whom Lucas could bully, since Abrams was far more experienced. Abrams was far from a household name for non-nerds, but since he had already directed a *Star Trek* film in addition to other feature films such as *Armageddon* and *Mission Impossible III*, he commanded a measure of respect and confidence.

Proof of Abrams's strong personality was on display when on November 30, 2015, while discussing *The Force Awakens* at a SiriusXM satellite radio town hall meeting, he was asked whether he believed Han had shot first—to which he responded, "Oh, hell yes."[2] Nevertheless, by all accounts, Abrams and Lucas enjoyed a warm friendship. In 2013, Jett Lucas, George Lucas's son, revealed that Abrams and his dad talked all the time.[3]

Lucas always maintained that he wanted other filmmakers to play in his *Star Wars* universe. In the past, he approached filmmakers such as David Lynch, Steven Spielberg, and Robert Zemeckis, but they all turned him down. Consequently, the directors who took the leap into the *Star Wars* universe were never big names who commanded a lot of respect. Bringing in blue-collar, expendable directors was more like the old Hollywood studio system than the American New Wave that Lucas helped create.

Lucas sat in on story sessions with Kasdan and the writing team at Disney and helped explain the rules of his universe. Lawrence Kasdan, presumably, needed no tutorial, having penned screenplays for both *The Empire Strikes Back* and *Return of the Jedi*.

In 2012, Kathleen Kennedy created a story group led by Kiri Zooper Hart and Leland Chee, who were tasked with keeping track of all *Star Wars* content and maintaining Lucas's vision. One of the first things the story group did was eliminate the Expanded Universe or EU, designating everything other than the films and television shows, like *The Clone Wars* and *Star Wars: Rebels*, as *Star Wars* "Legends," effectively relegating noncanonical work to an apocryphal or unverified status. This included the novels by Timothy Zahn, some of the characters of which, like Grand Admiral Thrawn, had already become canonized by appearing in *Star Wars: Rebels*. This was another slap in the face of fans, similar to Lucas's attempts to shut down fan fiction decades earlier. The EU was largely the creation of fans who weathered the dormant years of the *Star Wars* franchise in between the first two trilogies, which kept things pumping and interest levels up. Kennedy and the story group rebooted or retconned the franchise, eliminating large swathes of material, not unlike the Death Star eliminating entire planets. There was essentially no good reason for Kennedy and Lucasfilm to do this. There was already an established hierarchy whereby fans privileged what appeared in the films or television shows, even if it contradicted what was in the books or other artifacts. By announcing the severance of the EU, Lucasfilm only succeeded in, once again, alienating fans.

When the story group eliminated thirty years of *Star Wars* lore, they pushed the franchise one step closer to the brink of irrelevance. This was an ill-advised move that did not take into account that the number-one driver of *Star Wars* was the fans, not Disney and not Lucas. While Lucas always admitted that he was not beholden to the EU, he never outright disavowed it either. Nothing really changed. It was all just rhetoric. The announcement signaled that Lucasfilm Disney was willing to do whatever it wanted to in relation to the characters, regardless of what other writers had done. While other writers may have created narratives in which Han and Leia had twins, to Lucasfilm Disney it did not matter. It never mattered anyway, really, only it was never codified as not mattering.

In some cases, Lucasfilm simply co-opted fans such as Pablo Hidalgo, who wound up writing for one of the first *Star Wars* roleplaying games. In 2000, Lucasfilm hired Hidalgo as an internet content developer and tasked him with managing *starwars.com*. Hidalgo also wrote extensively for the *Star Wars* Encyclopedia. Lucasfilm called on him to help shepherd Disney through the *Star Wars* universe before Disney bought the franchise.

Not long after the sale of Lucasfilm to Disney, George Lucas became engaged to a woman of color named Mellody Hobson, the president of Ariel Investments and chair of DreamWorks animation. The two already had a child on the way via a surrogate mother. On August 9, 2013, Lucas's surrogate delivered their baby, Everest Hobson Lucas. It was Lucas's first biological child. The details of George's biological relationship with his new daughter were sketchy, but likely the couple used some form of in-vitro fertilization, whereby quality sperm was separated and introduced to the egg manually. The only way to collect a semen sample in this scenario is for the male partner to masturbate, often in the care of an embryologist at a fertility center with the aid of a special nontoxic lubricant. Presumably, a sixty-nine-year-old Lucas masturbated at a fertility center, and the resultant semen was used to impregnate the surrogate woman. The optics of George Lucas having a child through technological means as opposed to natural sex is oddly in keeping with what we know about the man. Lucas was never a romantic man; it was clear that he and his first wife, Marcia, did not enjoy a robust sex life. Even at USC, his friends joked that Lucas was not much of a lady's man. On top of that, his films have all been devoid of positive images of sexuality. Notably, a recurrent image in George Lucas's films is of a dancing, scantily clad black woman. Lucas eschewed character for plot, and was more interested in effects than actors. The romantic scenes between Anakin and Padme were perhaps some of the worst in all of *Star Wars*. The dialogue was stiff, melodramatic, and lifeless, as though written by someone who had never experienced passionate love. It made perfect sense that Lucas would have his first biological child through technological means. There was no other way for the famed creator of *Star Wars*. In making films as well as babies, George Lucas was closer to a droid than a human.

One hiccup along the way for Disney was the departure of screenwriter Michael Arndt, who was attached to *Episode VII* even before Kasdan and Abrams but left the project under mysterious circumstances. Rumors swirled that, like Lucas, Arndt bristled at the idea of focusing *Episode VII* on old characters instead of new ones. Disney attempted to deflect any bad or negative press by releasing positive news, such as the hiring of John Williams to create the score.

Disney President Alan Horn discussed *Episode VII* for the first time on April 17, 2013, at CinemaCon. While he spoke, a surveillance system called PirateEye scanned the audience for anyone recording his comments with a smart phone. Security teams with night-vision goggles patrolled the crowd during Horn's presentation. Horn told the audience that the plan was for Disney to release a *Star Wars* film every year, with spinoffs coming in between the episodes.[4] This was the first time that anyone at Disney actually articulated the idea that there would be a *Star Wars* film released *every year*. Considering there had only been six over the last four decades, the notion of a *Star Wars* film every year was a huge change and a huge risk. There was evidence that Horn and Kennedy were not seeing eye to eye. Horn cited a release date for *Episode VII* in the summer of 2015. Kennedy was more cautious.

Kennedy also announced that *Episode VII* would use puppets and models in addition to CGI. She directed the announcement at the legions of fans who criticized the prequels as too antiseptic, too technological at the expense of flesh and bone. Kennedy asserted that they would use every tool at their disposal, including non-CGI related effects. She conveyed that if they did not respect the foundation of the stories, the original style, and come up with unique narratives, the work would get stale.[5] Kennedy's comments appeared to reference Lucas's overuse of CGI and blue screens in the prequels as well as the tendency of *Star Wars* films to revisit hackneyed plots such as the destruction of the Death Star. Many of the plans for *Episode VII* were seemingly in direct response to Lucas's perceived failures in relation to the prequels—that he used too much CGI, that he alienated his older fans. Perhaps the well was already tainted. Maybe *Star Wars* had lost the fans.

Ironically, *Star Wars* fans hated *Star Wars*, hated it so much that they consumed it at record levels in order to fuel that hate. What Disney stood to lose beyond this paradox was actual ticket sales. *Star Wars* had always made money regardless of fan venom. Who knew whether this paradoxical track record would continue?

In November 2014, Disney CEO Bob Iger, Kennedy, and Abrams released the title of the seventh *Star Wars* film, *The Force Awakens*. As with previous titles, fans immediately and obsessively interrogated the title for clues. The new leadership ran the same sort of tight ship that Lucasfilm had under George Lucas. By winter of 2015, it seemed as though *Star Wars* was back in the popular collective mind as it had been for much of the last four decades.

In 2015, *Forbes* listed Lucas as the ninety-fourth richest American, with an estimated worth of $5 billion. He sheepishly responded to the listing by pointing out that he never cared about money, and that the only reason he made so much was so he could have creative control of his films.[6] Kennedy offered Lucas a private screening of the film in early December 2015. Lucas's private screening of *The Force Awakens* was telling on a number of counts. First was in relation to his declaration years earlier that he regretted being the only nerd who could not stand in line to see the next *Star Wars* film. This was bogus—he did not wait in line. There was no way George Lucas could be just a regular fan, a regular nerd. He rejected that membership long ago.

The other idea that the screening and his subsequent reaction undermined had to do with his reason for selling the franchise to Disney—that he was interested in seeing other directors play in his universe. Lucas's reticence about *The Force Awakens* indicated his disappointment, since a strong reaction would have helped drum up excitement for the film, resulting in a better box office, something one would think Lucas would welcome considering his large stake in the company. Kennedy related Lucas's reaction to the press sometime afterward, conveying that he really liked it. When later pressed, George admitted that he thought fans would love it and that it was exactly the kind of film they were looking for, which, on its face, was not exactly high praise in light of his relationship with *Star Wars* fandom.[7] Given Lucas's volatile relationship with *Star Wars* fans in general—the real reason why he sold the franchise—this response was telling. Clearly, Lucas did not like the film.

The truth eventually came out that Disney ignored Lucas's treatments and instead opted to make a story created by Kasdan, Arndt, and Abrams. The treatments that Lucas and Iger haggled over, the ones that Iger said had a lot of potential, were dismissed. On Christmas Day 2015, Lucas told Charlie Rose that Disney had decided that it was not interested in his story treatments for subsequent *Star Wars* films and that the company intended to do its own thing.[8] Rumors suggested that part of Lucas's vision for a new trilogy involved the microbiotic world of the midichlorians and the Whills, beings who control the universe, perhaps similar to the father, son, and daughter featured in season 3 of *The Clone Wars* when Anakin, Obi-Wan, and Ahsoka are stranded on the planet Amortis.

There was friction setting in between Lucas and Kennedy. Kennedy was no longer beholden to her former boss, but to her new boss, Bob Iger. Lucas was not involved in the making of *The Force Awakens* in any significant way. Kennedy later publicly stated that she felt George would not be happy unless he was 100 percent running the show, implying that her reason for excluding him was his need for control.[9]

Lucas put up a good front, even telling *USA Today* that he planned to see the film in a theater without knowing what was going to happen. This, of course, did not happen. Lucas likened watching Disney *Star Wars* films to attending his child's wedding and having to deal with his ex-wife. Likening Disney to his ex-wife Marcia, with whom he experienced one of the worst traumas in his life when he found out that she was involved with another man, an artist working on Skywalker Ranch, was odd. The comment indicated that he was bitter about the sale, to say the least.

Lucas criticized *The Force Awakens* as being a throwback movie that expressly catered to the fans. When Lucas saw the film, he realized why Iger and Abrams did not want him involved. If he were involved, there would have been conflict, which was not good for anyone.[10] Implicit in Lucas's criticism was the notion that Disney sold out and created a film with no vision except for making the fans happy, a retro film that brought back old characters and tried to help older fans recapture the childhood magic they failed to regain by watching the prequels. These sorts of criticisms were old hat for the franchise and would be levelled again and again in the films to come.

The last thing George Lucas was interested in was making movies that only catered to the fans. Lucas abandoned the internet entirely due to the toxicity of the fans, pointing to the fact that fans played a large role in Lucas selling the *Star Wars* franchise. He simply could not take the criticism anymore. It became too much.

Notwithstanding Lucas's lukewarm reception, *The Force Awakens* broke nearly every box office record in December 2015 on its way to making over $2 billion globally. Disney leaked plans for *Episode VIII* to be released in 2017 and *Episode IX* in 2019, as well as the spinoff films *Rogue One* and *Solo*, slated for release in the year in between these films.

Lucas told Jon Stewart that *Star Wars* snuck up on him and completely turned his life around and that coming to terms with its popularity was a very slow and arduous process.[11] In more than one interview, Lucas compared his situation to that of Darth Vader, trapped unwillingly by the inner workings of a technological empire, a metaphor that also linked fans to Luke Skywalker.[12]

The first weekend of the film's release, beginning on December 18, 2015, *The Force Awakens* grossed an estimated $238 million in the United States and Canada, breaking the record once again for the largest opening weekend. The film played in more than 4,000 theaters across the United States. It became the first film to break the $100 million mark in one single day.

Lucasfilm Disney released *Episode VII* in the heat of the 2016 presidential debates that would eventually lead to the election of Donald J. Trump. Hillary Clinton ended her closing statement at one of the Democratic debates by saying to viewers, "May the force be with you." Even President Barack Obama wrapped up one of his press conferences by saying he needed to get to *Star Wars*. By all indications, Disney had once again nailed it.

However, some critics, including *Los Angeles Times* columnist Michael Hiltzik, were not so enamored with Disney's take on the *Star Wars* universe. Hiltzik wondered why so many of the reviews, even the positive ones, seemed a little sad. His answer was because *The Force Awakens* was not very good and a rip-off of Lucas's first film, *A New Hope*. He criticized the film for being dull and unimaginative and reproducing the original film almost to the point of plagiarism.[13] The issue for Hiltzik was that *The Force Awakens* was not really a film as much as it was a product designed for mass appeal. The real injustice seemed to be the overt marketing of the film in relation to the toys, collectibles, theme park rides, video games, TV spinoffs, clothing, and promotional tie-ins, a criticism that Lucas received back in the 1970s.

Anne Friedman from the *Los Angeles Times* wrote an article on December 23, 2015, that tried to explain why she had just spent $30 to go see a film in which she was not that interested. Her answer was because it was a cultural phenomenon and nothing more. She admitted that she went to see *The Force Awakens* only because everyone else had.[14] For Friedman, the driving force behind her attendance in the theater was similar to why many kids saw the film back in 1977: because everyone else had. In the age of social media, the lingua franca of the new hit television show or must-see film was even more overwhelming than in decades past when it seemed as though everyone had seen a film or television show and was talking about it. No one wanted to be left out of water-cooler talk. The feeling could be alienating, driving one to see a film or binge-watch a show that one ordinarily would ignore. *Game of Thrones* was the most recent example of this, a show that seemingly everyone had seen and was talking about online. A company like Disney or even the directors or actors did not drive the success of a film like *Star Wars*. The most important element was the passion of the fans themselves, who enjoyed unbelievable control in terms of how a film or television show was received.

The democratizing power of the internet has given fans never-before-seen power. In effect, fans can bully people into seeing a film or watching a show. The alternative is cultural illiteracy. On the other hand, fans can also bully consumers into not seeing a film by excoriating it online at every turn, effectively negatively branding a film and anyone who sees it. Fans brand themselves as devotees of a particular franchise, and that branding becomes part of their identity. This is nothing new in the world of fandom. The only part that is new is the degree of visibility, which in and of itself is very powerful. One major aspect of the triumph of nerd culture is its visibility and its perceived authority. Nerds can no longer be ignored. In their hands lies much of the fate of contemporary popular culture. The nerds have won.

The charge that *The Force Awakens* recreated the first *Star Wars* stems in part from the McGuffin of the first film, which is initially finding Obi-Wan, and then rescuing the princess and blowing up the Death Star. In *The Force Awakens*, the McGuffin is finding the map to Luke's whereabouts and Luke himself and then destroying the First Order's planet-killing solar weapon. The plots are similar enough to warrant comparison. When BB8 finds Rey, it is very similar to R2D2 finding Luke in *A New Hope*. Poe Dameron's wry sense of humor in the face of danger and Finn's greenness and naiveté evoke Han and Luke when they first make their respective appearances in the *Star Wars* universe. Kylo Ren's mask overtly references his grandfather, Darth Vader. The reference to Luke Skywalker as a possible myth, according to Rey, is interesting insofar as Disney's decision to cast the EU to the realm of myth. The reference to the Falcon as garbage also references *A New Hope*. Finn and Rey meeting up with Han and Chewie on the freighter strikingly resembles the Death Star sequence in *A New Hope*, complete with Rathtars resembling Dianoga. When discussing destroying the solar weapon of the First Order, one of the resistance fighters compares it to the Death Star.

What distinguishes *The Force Awakens* from *A New Hope* is the killing of Han Solo. This is perhaps the most brutal and coldblooded act of violence in all the *Star Wars* movies, if not the television shows—which are significantly more brutal than the films—and something Lucas would never have done even when Harrison Ford asked him to. This scene marks a transition touch point from Lucas to Disney. The film also introduces a new generation of heroes related to the Skywalkers and Palpatines. The blood smeared across Finn's Stormtrooper mask is another departure from a George Lucas–helmed franchise. More blood shows up on Poe's head as Kylo Ren tortures him for the map to the whereabouts of Luke Skywalker. Lucas was against there being any blood in his *Star Wars* movies. He was concerned about upsetting the children for whom his movies were made. His buddy Brian De Palma famously excoriated Lucas at an early screening of the first *Star Wars* film in the late 1970s because there was no blood in the film. Accusing *The Force Awakens* of mimicking *A New Hope* was not a new criticism for *Star Wars* filmmakers; George Lucas was criticized for the same thing when he made *Return of the Jedi*.

As Han Solo in *The Force Awakens* notes, "It's all true. Every bit of it." The first installment of the third trilogy and the first under the aegis of Disney is about believing again, believing in the force and believing in Disney's steward-ship. In a correction that undermined the role of midichlorians, the character Maz underscores the democratic nature of the force flowing through all living things, including a former Stormtrooper named Finn, whose force sensitivity is hinted at when he first clutches Luke's old lightsaber and then later deftly wields it against Kylo Ren. When Finn and Kylo square off with lightsabers, Finn holds his own, wounding Kylo's shoulder not unlike Luke wounding Darth Vader in *The Empire Strikes Back*. Han and Chewie save Finn while he battles Kylo, as they saved Luke many times in the past.

One person who was particularly upset about the death of Han Solo was Mark Hamill, who publicly lamented the killing of the character since that meant there would be no reunion of Han, Leia, and Luke. Hammill is both a major player in the *Star Wars* franchise as well as a fan. He qualified his opinion by noting that he realized it was self-centered. Hamill has emerged as a trusted voice of fandom online, representing a large swath of *Star Wars* fans in his dis-pleasure with the third trilogy's treatment of Han Solo and Luke Skywalker.[15]

The plan to release a new *Star Wars* film every year was a bold one. Part of what made *Star Wars* great was the anticipation, the delicious excitement between films when kids only had the toys to carry on the story. Part of the *Star Wars* experience was waiting in long lines. Fans for decades have enjoyed debating the plot developments for films that were never certain to come out. For Disney to give fans as much *Star Wars* as they could stomach was a move that changed the nature of the *Star Wars* experience. The first film to take that leap was *Rogue One*, slated for release in 2016, one year after *The Force Awakens*.

Lucasfilm Chief Creative Officer John Knoll came up with the idea for *Rogue One* when he was working on *Revenge of the Sith* and found out that Lucas was considering creating one-hour, live-action *Star Wars* television shows. Knoll thought one possible episode was the story of the group of rebels who stole the plans to the Death Star and delivered them to the Rebel Alliance while sustain-ing the great losses alluded to in the initial crawl of *A New Hope*. Knoll framed the story as a *Mission: Impossible* type of narrative. Seven years later, when Knoll found out that Lucas sold Lucasfilm to Disney and Kathleen Kennedy was considering stand-alone films, he approached Kennedy with his idea. It took some guts to pitch the story to Kennedy, who was leery of every *Star Wars* employee thinking they had a great idea for a film, but Kennedy was impressed right away with Knoll's idea. Kennedy told him up front that the stand-alone films had more freedom than previous films. Kennedy suggested that episodic films, either prequels or sequels, were restricted to a particular tone and style, while the stand-alone films had more freedom for experimentation. Kennedy's comments implied that the episodic films were more conservative in their story-telling. This was an inaccurate statement, considering that the films composing the original trilogy were wildly experimental and forced Industrial Light and Magic to literally invent the technology to achieve the effects Lucas insisted on, not to mention other Lucas innovations such as the "used universe" look and documentary style of shooting.

The feeling was that Disney needed to save *Star Wars* because Lucas had ruined it by alienating fans. Kennedy had already mentioned that the stand-alone *Solo* film to appear in 2017 would be more of a western. The idea of a space western being different from *A New Hope* is also inaccurate. The original films, especially *A New Hope*, were quintessential space westerns and were considered so at the time, especially in foreign markets like China where, before the films were even released, *Star Wars* books were available for Chinese consumers that depicted astronauts on horses.

Disney tapped director Gareth Edwards to direct *Rogue One*; two years earlier, he had directed *Godzilla 2014*. Edwards, a devout *Star Wars* fan, grew up in England and was inspired to be a filmmaker by George Lucas and his *Star Wars* films. For his thirtieth birthday, he made a pilgrimage to Tunisia to the old set of Tatooine and brought along food coloring so that he could drink blue milk like a real Jedi. Edwards admitted that he pushed the envelope with *Rogue One*.[16] He never thought that he would have the opportunity to make a *Star Wars* film. He thought Lucas would do them all. He felt like he was playing with house money and could push the envelope as far as he wished because the franchise was failure-proof and always made up the cost of the film, no matter what. In Edwards's mind, the more important task was maintaining the myth.

Edward's vision for *Rogue One* was for it to be a gritty, documentary-style war film, which just so happened to be George Lucas's identical vision for the original 1977 *Star Wars* film. In avoiding the perceived pitfalls of Lucas, Edwards and the story group at Disney wound up finding Lucas's original vision inspired by the French New Wave and truth cinema.

During reshoots for *Rogue One*, Lucasfilm Disney brought in director Tony Gilroy to bring the film across the finish line, something that never would have happened in the era of the New Hollywood when studios gave auteur filmmakers long leashes. Kennedy effectively benched Edwards. Gilroy would later say that the film was in serious trouble when he was brought in and paid $5 million

THIS IS THE WAY

to save it. Gilroy was not a fan of the franchise and had no reverence or qualms at all with killing off characters. At issue was the end of the film. Before Kennedy tapped Gilroy, Edwards had a few of the characters live, thinking that Disney would not allow everyone to die. Gilroy realized the film was about sacrifice and killed everyone off. There were extensive reshoots, which is why there are scenes in the trailer that do not appear in the actual film.[17] Edwards responded by saying that making a *Star Wars* film was a team sport, a team effort, and that *Rogue One* was no different. He also offered that if anyone should take credit for the film, it was George Lucas, not Edwards, Gilroy, or Disney.[18] From his perspective, *Star Wars* belonged to the world, and those in charge of *Rogue One* were just borrowing it.

According to John Knoll, Lucas called him just after he screened *Rogue One* to congratulate him and say that he was very pleased with the film. Lucas told Knoll that he thought the film looked gorgeous and matched his aesthetic perfectly, honoring his legacy.[19]

*Rogue One* premiered on December 16, 2016, and Lucasfilm Disney marketed it as the first spinoff film in the *Star Wars* franchise. *Chicago Tribune* writer Josh Rottenburg averred that *Rogue One* was the darkest *Star Wars* film since *The Empire Strikes Back* and put the "Wars" in *Star Wars*. He positively described the film as visceral and morally complex.[20]

There are innovations in *Rogue One* that set it apart from other *Star Wars* films, namely the moral complexity of the primary characters, such as Jane Erso and her father Galen Erso as well as Saw Gerrera. These are characters not easily categorized as rebels or members of the Empire's Imperial army. While Galen is instrumental in creating the Death Star, he is also instrumental in its destruction. Saw Gerrera, while not a rebel, is certainly not a member of the Empire. Even Cassian Andor and K2 are not clear heroes in the film. Andor's decision to assassinate Galen Erso is shrouded in moral ambiguity, and K2 is a reprogrammed Imperial droid.

By all measures, *Rogue One* was a smash hit, exceeding expectations and enjoying an opening of over $155 million in the United States and Canada. *Rogue One* recorded the second-highest December of any film except for *The Force Awakens* released the year before. It would go on to be the top-grossing film of 2016. As far as anyone could tell, with *Rogue One* and *The Force Awakens*, Disney was doing right by *Star Wars*. That would all change with *The Last Jedi* and *Solo: A Star Wars Story*. Disney had seized upon a winning strategy, giving the fans exactly what they wanted: more *Star Wars*.

There were rumors of more stand-alone films, including stories centered on characters like Boba Fett and Obi-Wan Kenobi as well as others. Lucas's playground was endless, or so it seemed. Perhaps Lucas's vision for *Star Wars* had come to pass. He had always talked about letting other directors take a shot at his franchise and that he was excited to see how others interpreted his world and what sorts of stories they came up with.

There were many tantalizing questions left unanswered at the end of *The Force Awakens*, the answers to which fans eagerly anticipated with *Episode VIII*. J. J. Abrams teed up the writer and director for the next film by withholding key elements of the story, such as the origins of Snoke, Rey, and the story behind Luke's lightsaber, not to mention the biggest storyline of all, Luke Skywalker's reaction to being found by Rey and the remaining rebels.

When Disney called on Rian Johnson to both write and direct *Episode VIII*, several media outlets were surprised. When the news broke, Johnson himself tweeted a clip from *The Right Stuff* where an astronaut mumbles to himself, "Please don't let me fuck this up."[21] For the most part, Johnson was a no-name. His previous directing credit was for a film called *Looper*. He had also directed a few episodes of the hit TV show, *Breaking Bad*.

It was not as though *Star Wars* enjoyed a long history of famous directors. Previous directors of *Star Wars* films not named George Lucas included Irvin Kershner, Richard Marquand, J. J. Abrams, and Gareth Edwards, hardly household names. According to Kennedy, she had Johnson in mind from the beginning when she was considering directors for *Star Wars* movies.

Just before production began, Lucas called Johnson and asked to meet him for dinner at 8:30 p.m. that very night. Johnson was visibly shaken by the invitation but nervously laughed and accepted his fate. Lucas's shadow was long.[22]

Not long after production began, Johnson received a coordinated tweet storm from Russian accounts, pleading with him not to kill General Hux, the leader of the First Order. Johnson was caught in a historical moment, a global vortex of forces that included George Lucas and a fandom that stretched the circumference of the globe.

Johnson's vision for the film focused on attempting to figure out exactly what happened right after *The Force Awakens*. In Johnson's mind, Luke was a reluctant Jedi who refused to be the sort of hero Rey, fans, and especially Mark Hamill wanted him to be.

From Hamill's perspective, he did not own the character; the character belonged to the fans. The difference in visions between Rian Johnson and Mark Hamill was a microcosm of the fight between Lucas and fans of the film since its genesis. Mark Hamill as an actor had no more right to impose his vision onto the character as fans had the right to impose theirs. *Star Wars* instilled in people very strong emotions and convictions with regard to the characters and the story, convictions that seemed worth fighting for and crying over.

Johnson was interested in subverting fan expectations for the film. This included characterization, casting, and plot. For example, Johnson wanted fans to associate Benicio Del Toro's character DJ with Han Solo, a sort of rogue with a heart of gold, and then undermine that expectation by having DJ betray the rebel alliance.

*The Last Jedi* functioned as a goodbye not only to Carrie Fisher but also to George Lucas. Whereas *The Force Awakens* and *Rogue One* owed heavy debts to *A New Hope*, *The Last Jedi* was truly a different sort of vision with a different sort of director, whose intentions were to undermine audience expectations and take the *Star Wars* franchise in a completely new direction, making good on Lucas's promise decades earlier that he would make the franchise available for new visions and new voices.

In subverting the expectations of fans, Johnson also subverted the expectations of the film's biggest star, Mark Hamill. This alone was reason enough for fans to hate *The Last Jedi* even more than the prequels. For Rian Johnson, the character that excited him the most was not Luke but rather Kylo Ren. Ren gave him the opportunity to make evil relatable. Even though Vader was a tremendous villain in the originals, he was not easily relatable, according to Johnson.[23] Johnson's instincts appear to have been on point with respect to the possibilities of Kylo Ren, played by a nearly unknown actor named Adam Driver, who a few years later would be the hottest leading man in all of Hollywood.

Making the film new involved returning to techniques that Lucas used because he did not have the technology to achieve the effects that he desired. For example, Johnson made the decision to re-create Yoda as a puppet with Frank Oz, rather than create him with CGI.

Other examples of Johnson subverting expectations were in relation to some of the gags in the film, such as Poe Dameron prank-calling General Hux and the presentation of Canto Bight as a hyper-capitalist, exploitative war industry built on the exploitation of animals and children. *The Last Jedi*'s Marxist context in this sequence harkens back to George Lucas and his original desire to democratize filmmaking for filmmakers and take over the means of production, similar to Anakin's original vow against the Dark Side and the Sith, which he ultimately and spectacularly broke.

The most promising sequence in *The Last Jedi* involves the exploited children of Canto Bight and the implication that they will compose the next generation of Jedi. In this sequence, the children play with the same toys that drew most *Star Wars* fans in—and very likely including Rian Johnson. Their play leads to their power. This is a genuflection to the fans and a massive indication of the democratization of the force. Further subversions of fan expectations include Kylo's killing of Snoke but refusal to join the rebels, Rey's modest origins, and Luke astrally projecting himself before becoming a force ghost.

In 2017 Scott Mendelson, a senior film contributor to *Forbes* magazine, noted that despite the good reviews, good box office gross, and good audience polling, there was a feeling in the air that a large segment of *Star Wars* fans hated *The Last Jedi*.[24] Mendelson cited the unusually low audience score on the popular *Rotten Tomatoes* (rottentomatoes.com), a website that provides aggregate response scores from critics as well as fans. The critical aggregate score for *The Last Jedi* certified the film fresh with a 91 percent, meaning that 91 percent of critics thought positively of the film, while the audience score was a very low 44 percent. Some argued that a small segment of *Star Wars* fans had artificially deflated the score. On the other hand, *The Force Awakens* had a critical aggregate score of 92 percent and an audience score of 87 percent. By further comparison, *Rogue One*'s critical score was 84 percent and its audience score was 86 percent. The much-maligned first prequel, *The Phantom Menace*, scored 54 and 59 percent respectively. The much-vaunted *The Empire Strikes Back* came in at 95 and 97. The *Star Wars* movie with the lowest critical and audience scores was *The Clone Wars*, with aggregate scores of 18 and 39 percent respectively. There was something going on with *The Last Jedi*. Rian Johnson had pissed off a lot of fans. His vision of letting old legends die did not sit well with the bread and butter of the franchise.

Abrams asked audiences to remember. Johnson asked audiences to forget, to forget the Jedi and to embrace the new characters and the democratic nature of the force. Abrams killed Solo. Johnson killed Luke. Luke makes an argument that the rise of the Empire was due to the hubris of the Jedi and suggests the legend of the Jedi is a myth. Johnson through Kylo Ren urges Rey and *Star Wars* audiences to let the past die, to kill it if they have to in order to make room for new storylines and new characters. While Abrams spent much of the first film trying to invoke the past, Johnson spent much of the second film trying to kill it. Abrams would double down on his efforts with the third film of the third trilogy, to disastrous effects.

In the context of *Star Wars* fans rejecting Johnson's bold moves in *The Last Jedi*, one could argue that *Solo: A Star Wars Story* never had a chance. Not only did Disney double down on the idea of releasing a *Star Wars* film every year, but this time they only waited five months. *Star Wars* fans had not yet digested *The Last Jedi*, a film that self-consciously played with their expectations like no other

*Star Wars* film had. It was too soon. Fans needed time to process the trauma and channel their frustration that Rian Johnson had consciously courted.

In a move forecasted by what took place on the set of *Rogue One*, when one director was benched and another brought in to finish the film, in June 2017 Lucasfilm Disney fired directors Phil Lord and Chris Miller and brought in Ron Howard as the new director of the upcoming *Solo*, featuring the origin story of one of the most beloved characters in the franchise. Lord and Miller, known for their quirky and irreverent humor, were the directors of *The LEGO Movie* as well as *Cloudy with a Chance of Meatballs*. After having been on set for four and a half months and shooting three-quarters of principal photography, their firing was announced and described as due to major creative differences between the directing duo and Kathleen Kennedy and Lawrence Kasdan.

The two Dartmouth directors were interested in making the film more of a comedy and going off Kasdan's script. This was an example of young, fresh directors *not* being given carte blanche when it came to eating at the table of the *Star Wars* franchise. Lucasfilm Disney increasingly demonstrated that it was not open to new and fresh directorial takes on the *Star Wars* universe, despite previous pronouncements. Perhaps Lucasfilm believed that giving Johnson the freedom to innovate was a bad idea after all and was not about to make the same mistake with Lord and Miller. The company's moves were reminiscent of old Hollywood, a time when the executives in the big studios thought directors were a dime a dozen and expendable—the very system that motivated George Lucas to create Lucasfilm. All of a sudden, like Anakin's turn to the dark side and subsequent terrorizing of the galaxy, Lucas had created what he vowed to destroy: a studio that cared little about its directors and their unique visions.

Picking Ron Howard to take over was a no-brainer. A longtime friend of Lucas who appeared in his first major film *American Graffiti*, not only did Howard already have a connection with the corporation, but he was also a proven commodity and a bankable director. Perhaps he and his ilk were actually whom George Lucas had in mind when he suggested that he was interested in other directorial visions for the franchise. Kennedy's press release in relation to hiring Ron Howard referenced carrying forward the spirit of the saga and George Lucas.[25]

Lucas had asked Howard to direct *The Phantom Menace* after Robert Zemeckis and Steven Spielberg said no, but Howard declined as well, noting that nobody wanted to touch the prequels because everyone wanted George to do them.[26]

Until *Solo: A Star Wars Story*, Disney's efforts to continue the long-running space opera series were virtually unassailable. Disney's first three *Star Wars* movies, starting in 2015 with *The Force Awakens*, paid off handsomely for the entertainment giant. *Solo: A Star Wars Story* premiered on May 10, 2018, only five months after the premier of *The Last Jedi*. Whether due to *Star Wars* fatigue or the shuffling of directors, *Solo* was the least successful *Star Wars* movie of all time. One lingering fear was that some fans were still *luke*-warm, if not outright enraged, by *The Last Jedi* and that their online grousing dampened excitement for *Solo*, which grossed $84 million in its first three days in theaters, missing analyst expectations during Memorial Day weekend. In another troubling sign, the movie collected $29 million domestically in its second weekend, represent-ing a steep 65 percent tumble from its opening.

In the first couple of weeks, the prequel about the adventures of a young Han Solo grossed about $264 million worldwide, including $149 million in the United States and Canada, significantly lagging behind the previous movies. While some folks thought the tepid sales for *Solo* was a one-off, others worried it signaled that *Star Wars* had grown stale.[27]

The notion of franchise fatigue stemmed from the lack of a cooling-off period between films. There had been a year between each of the previous three *Star Wars* films but a decade between the last of the prequels and *The Force Awak-ens*. The first and second trilogy were separated by sixteen years. Even the first three films in the *Star Wars* franchise were separated by three years. Lucas used that same pace for the prequels. The problem was that, as far as Disney was concerned, *Star Wars* was a bankable commodity—and the thing to do with a bankable commodity is bank it. However, there was a feeling in the air that fans were finally sick of *Star Wars*, that they had overdosed on the franchise.

International numbers were equally lackluster. The movie grossed $115 mil-lion outside the United States and Canada, including $15 million in China, a key box office market where the series had failed to catch on. Analysts expected the film eventually to amass about $450 million in worldwide box office revenue, far lower than *Rogue One*.

Once *Solo* opened to a lackluster box office based on the unusual standards of a *Star Wars* franchise, many rushed to figure out what happened, and plenty of folks offered advice for Disney to ensure that the franchise stayed strong and healthy. One piece of advice that Steven Zeitchik of the *Washington Post* offered Disney and Lucasfilm was to tell edgier stories.[28]

Director Ron Howard ascribed the poor box office performance to what he called "trolls," or anti-fans. According to Howard, the hardcore fans went to see the film, but the film failed to capture mainstream audiences because of the trolls.[29] While *Solo* generated nearly $400 million worldwide, its nearly $500 million production cost put the film in the red. Mark Hamill suggested that fans were afflicted with *Star Wars* fatigue.[30]

The advent of the internet and the sheer ability to crowdsource assessments of any given film has reduced the power of film critics like Pauline Kael, who was so influential in Hollywood among the American New Wave directors in the 1970s. A large swath of the public who make their voices heard on the internet has filled this void. What has emerged, particularly in the universe of *Star Wars*, might be called the anti-fan. The anti-fan is one who actively and vocally hates a given cultural production. These trolls seem to derive pleasure from trashing a film or show. Typically and historically, critics have tried to distance themselves from that which they were assessing, attempting to make a sober assessment of a work of art whether they loved or hated it. Loving fans, on the other hand, make no apologies for their love for a production when they assess it. Anti-fans are neither critics nor loving fans. They are the inverse of loving critics. They hate unconditionally.[31]

Similar to *Rogue One*, *Solo* lacked the familiar opening crawl, marking it as a stand-alone film and not part of a trilogy. While it would not have been plausible to number the stand-alone films as episodes since it would affect the numbering of the other episodes, there was no reason why the stand-alone films needed to be stylistically different, especially since they both seamlessly fit within the main narrative. The lack of the familiar crawl ghettoized the films and made them feel unnecessary and extra.

Both *Rogue One* and *Solo* were deeply enmeshed in the cultural fabric of *Star Wars*. For example, the opening sequence depicting a young Han boosting a speeder directly evokes a young George Lucas and his first love of cars and situates Han as a doppelganger of Lucas, as he was in *A New Hope*. True to form, although the film starts as a potential love story, that plot strand quickly dissolves, mirroring George Lucas's fraught history with love. After being separated in the first ten minutes of the film, three years later Han finds Qi'ra working for Dryden Vos as a sort of sex slave and first lieutenant. Echoing the Exogorth and the Sarlacc, as well as many other creatures resembling monstrous genitalia in the *Star Wars* universe, *Solo* features a giant vaginal maw that threatens Han Solo and his crew on the Millennium Falcon. There are other vestiges of Lucas in the film, such as a black female entertainer performing at Dryden Voss's place, echoing scenes from both *THX 1138* and *The Empire Strikes Back*.

Evidence of the thumbprint of Phil Lord and Chris Miller include references to Lando Calrissian's penis and his romantic relationship with his droid R-3, which borders on farce. *Solo*'s charm lies in its depiction of the underbelly of the galaxy, arguably more convincingly done in *The Clone Wars* television series. These are the thieves and rogues of the galaxy, operating on a lower substratum than the characters in *Rogue One* who were neither rebels nor part of the Empire, but rather high-minded activists and extremists who figured mightily in the plans of both the rebellion and the Empire. The characters in *Solo* have risen from the slums and only figure in the narrative of the galaxy through grit and luck. Perhaps the most important scene in all of *Solo* is Han shooting Beckett, a direct response to Lucas's alteration of the Han and Greedo scene in *A New Hope*.

On April 12, 2019, the first tantalizing preview for *Episode IX: The Rise of Skywalker* dropped. The trailer signaled the return of Lando Calrissian, Luke Skywalker, and the Emperor. Reports from the set of *The Rise of Skywalker* from actors such as Daisy Ridley reassured fans that they would be very satisfied with the ending of the film rumored to end the Skywalker saga. There were also online rumors that Disney consulted with George Lucas about the film. In addition to *The Rise of Skywalker* getting ready for release, Disney was also about to launch their streaming service Disney+, for which they had been developing original content such as the live action show *The Mandalorian*, featuring Pedro Pascal as the titular bounty hunter, Din Djarin. Published reports confirmed that series creator, *Avengers* and *Iron Man* director Jon Favreau, sought advice from Lucas, publicly noting that they had a long talk about the show that takes place five years after *Return of the Jedi*. According to Favreau, Lucas emphasized that the audience has always been the kids who are coming of age, a strict philosophy that has caused Lucas endless amounts of grief.[32]

*The Mandalorian* was not fifty-four-year-old Jon Favreau's first rodeo in relation to the *Star Wars* franchise. The actor and director, famous for such films as *Swingers* and for his wildly popular *Iron Man* films, provided the voice of the Mandalorian Pre Vizsla in *The Clone Wars* and the Ardennian pilot Rio Durant in *Solo: A Star Wars Story*. He also provided the voice for Paz Vizla in *The Mandalorian*. A longtime *Star Wars* fan, his appearance in *The Clone Wars* was due to running into Dave Filoni at ILM and Skywalker Sound while Favreau was working on postproduction for *Iron Man*. Favreau was an example of the triumph of nerd culture, a fan who successfully made the canonical leap from fan creative to *Star Wars* creator.

An early review of *The Mandalorian* by Zaki Hasan for an online publication called *Datebook* posted on November 15, 2019, cautioned legions of fans who were in love with the series from the moment the first episode aired on Disney+. Hasan pointed out that a familiar cycle in *Star Wars* reception had been wild approval, followed by sober reappraisal that often devolved into vicious attack.[33]

No other *Star Wars* installment enjoyed such wide and immediate acclaim as *The Mandalorian*. Debuting in the fall of 2019, less than two months before the premier of *The Rise of Skywalker*, the aggregate score for the series was 95 percent critical approval and 93 percent audience approval, slightly higher than the stellar score for *The Clone Wars* television series and a higher critical score than *The Empire Strikes Back*.

The series premiered on the heels of *The Last Jedi* and *Solo: A Star Wars Story*, two films that many thought spelled doom for the franchise, one because of Rian Johnson's subversive vision for a fan base that was not interested in being subverted, and the other because it was the first franchise film to qualify as a flop. In that sense, the timing of *The Mandalorian* could not have been better.

The protagonist, Din Djarin, owes a huge debt to the first *Star Wars* Mandalorian, Boba Fett, who rose to stardom in the first trilogy despite limited screen time and an unceremonious ending in *Return of the Jedi* when he seemingly dies in the Sarlacc Pit in the desert of Tatooine. Lucas tasked the character with carrying much of the narrative of the prequels, as Jango Fett, Boba Fett's father, is the template for the Republic's Clone Army. The Mandalorians also figure strongly in *The Clone Wars* television series, as many of the best story arcs take place on the planet Mandalore.

The very first scene in *The Mandalorian* positions the show squarely within the genre of steampunk western as the lone warrior hunter enters a dangerous saloon where he his immediately accosted and must demonstrate his fighting skills. There is an element of noir as well, as Mando is also an investigator of sorts, a bounty hunter forced to operate in a liminal space somewhere outside the law. He is neither criminal nor law-abiding. He lives by the code of the Mandalorians as well as the code of the bounty hunter guild. He is not easily bribed and never takes off his helmet in front of another living thing. He is deeply principled, if not lawful. The world of the Mandalorian is the underbelly of the *Star Wars* universe, a world even below that of *Solo*. These are the economic bottom feeders of a world torn apart by the destruction of the Empire.

*The Mandalorian* takes place five years after the events in *Return of the Jedi* and the death of Emperor Palpatine and Darth Vader. Grimy Stormtroopers and ruthless bounty hunters, some of whom were first introduced in *The Empire Strikes Back*, populate the show. A recurring character is Kuiil, an Ugnaught voiced by Nick Nolte, a species first introduced in *The Empire Strikes Back* as workers who set up the carbonite-freezing chamber. Kuiil assists Djarin in locating his most important quarry.

Perhaps the biggest moment in *Star Wars* history since Darth Vader revealed his paternity to Luke Skywalker was when audiences first laid eyes on Baby

Yoda. In the show, Din Djarin agrees to deliver an important quarry to an evil splinter group that was once part of the Empire. The important quarry turns out to be a baby resembling Yoda. Despite receiving a handsome bounty for Baby Yoda, Djarin undergoes an extreme change of heart and breaks his bounty hunter guild code in order to rescue Baby Yoda once he realizes that the baby is in danger. This places the Mandalorian at odds with the remaining vestiges of the empire as well as the bounty hunters' guild, the governing body responsible for his livelihood. He is a true outlaw, an outlaw of outlaws, who follows a higher code. As a result, Mando emerges as a sort of father figure for Baby Yoda, endearing him to a fandom made up of both men and women.

Almost immediately, memes of Baby Yoda began popping up all over the internet. Never mind that there was no plausible way the baby could actually be Yoda, who is 900 years old in *Return of the Jedi* and dies on screen. Nevertheless, the minute Baby Yoda appeared on screen, balance was restored to the force. Disney hit it out of the park with the first *Star Wars* live-action series and the flagship show for Disney+.

Writing for *Forbes*, senior contributor Erik Kain offered that *The Mandalorian* was his favorite *Star Wars* release since *Return of the Jedi*. For Kain, a *Star Wars* fan, *The Mandalorian* was the best production since the original trilogy. He noted the dirty armor and demoralized attitude of the beleaguered Stormtroopers post-Empire. He also asserted that for the first time, fans were able to see the *Star Wars* universe from a different perspective.[34]

Two months before the premier of *The Rise of Skywalker*, an old ghost from *Star Wars* past emerged and brought everyone back to the 1970s and the American New Wave. Martin Scorsese once again made news by lamenting the dominance of big-budget films over smaller, more personal independent films. Once again, he directed his ire at his old friend and rival, George Lucas. While Scorsese technically lobbed shade at Marvel, it was very difficult to read Scorsese's gripes irrespective of Lucasfilm, since Disney owned both companies.

Scorsese quipped that Marvel movies and, by implication, *Star Wars* movies were more like theme parks than films.[35] This criticism was reminiscent of early critics of Lucas who called him a toymaker rather than a filmmaker, which Lucas took as a compliment since he said that if he were not a filmmaker he would *be* a toymaker. As a huge fan of Disney and one of the kids who attended Disneyland when it first opened, likening Lucas's films to theme parks or rides in theme parks was not shade. It was praise.

Scorsese offered that Marvel films were not cinema. For Scorsese, cinema was about revelation: aesthetic, emotional, and spiritual, vis-à-vis the paradoxes and flaws inherent in the human condition. For Scorsese, cinema was about risk. He noted that when he first began making movies along with Lucas and the other members of the New Hollywood, he was exposed to *real* movies. He noted that he and his friends, presumably including Lucas, often had to defend film as an art-form and that Marvel movies disrespected that fight by not making art films. Where Marvel fell short, according to Scorcese, was in terms of revelation and risk. Marvel movies were made with no risk involved. They were market-driven and market-proof. Scorcese's comments echoed his comments four decades earlier when he said that *Star Wars* had taken all the chips off the table in 1977. His comments, if nothing else, were an interesting reminder of the history of the *Star Wars* franchise and Scorcese and Lucas's personal history.

*Star Wars: The Rise of Skywalker* opened on December 20, 2019, to mixed reviews. It seemed as though fans had finally gotten more *Star Wars* than they knew what to do with. With the ninth feature film in the Skywalker saga, *Star Wars* had finally become just another franchise. The film suffered enormously from thematic overkill in relation to life and death. In attempting to appease older fans, Abrams decided to resurrect old characters, whether they were dead or alive. The film is populated by ghosts, including a performance by an actress who was literally dead during filming. The decision to feature Princess Leia as a major character despite the death of Carrie Fisher gave the film a farcical quality that added to the shaky logic of the return of the Emperor. Add to that the death and rebirth of Chewbacca, C3PO, and Han Solo, not as a force ghost but rather as a sort of waking ghost or apparition, and the movie undermined what makes life precious, which is to say, death. Layered alongside the inconsistencies due to opposing directorial visions between Johnson and Abrams, the third trilogy rates a distant third behind the other two trilogies. Lucas largely drove the first two trilogies. For better or worse, those trilogies were coherent in their storytelling.

*The Rise of Skywalker* picked up where the first film left off and nearly ignored the second film, or tried to revise it. The result was a very unsatisfying third film full of cameos and nods to the past with precious little plot, new characters, or risk of any kind. The first three lines of the initial crawl are "The dead speak," a reference to the overall theme of resurrection in the film, not only of characters but also of Abrams's vision for the third trilogy that was hijacked by Rian Johnson.

In a development that was forecasted in *The Mandalorian* when Baby Yoda demonstrates his force healing ability in an early episode, Rey demonstrates her force healing ability first on an underground sand burrowing monster called a Vexis snake and then on Kylo Ren himself. The first instance is significant in that it is the first time a phallic or vaginal monster is tamed by a character in the franchise, not insignificantly, by a woman. Rey's power with the force is unmatched as she is able to pull a ship from the sky. In addition to the deaths and resurrection of the Emperor, C3PO, Chewbacca, Han Solo, and the extra-textual rebirth of Carrie Fisher as Princess Leia, the climax of the film features the death and rebirth of both Kylo Ren and Rey.

Brian Lowry, the day after the film premiered in the United States, published one of the first reviews of *The Rise of Skywalker* on CNN's website. While the title of the review was "*Star Wars: The Rise of Skywalker* Rises to the Occasion of Concluding the Epic Saga," the review itself was not very positive at all and touched on why the movie actually failed rather than rose to the occasion of ending the Skywalker saga.

Lowry admonished Disney Lucasfilm for allowing opposing artistic visions to split its baby apart. Lowry noted that the film was more interested in a course correction than being a great film. He further noted that there were very few new characters and that the film's plot treaded on old narrative lines like choosing one's own path and destroying world-killing technology. The story was not inventive but rather interested in rekindling nostalgia.[36]

Bob Grimm spared no feelings in his review titled "A Spent Force: The End of the *Star Wars* Saga Stinks Like a Womp Rat's Ass" that appeared in the *Tucson Weekly* the day after Christmas.[37] Grimm called the film a rancid turd in the first line of his review; he was clearly upset. He noted, as did Lowry, that the first hour was unwatchable because the editing was too fast and seemed as though the creators were making it up as they went along. He trashed the choice to include Fisher and compared the trilogy unfavorably to the previous two. Grimm noted that *The Rise of Skywalker* was an apology for the much superior preceding film, *The Last Jedi*. In trying to win back fans who hated *The Last Jedi*, Abrams and Lucasfilm Disney laid an egg.

The aggregate audience score for *The Rise of Skywalker* on Rotten Tomatoes was 86 percent fresh with a very low critics score of 52 percent, which represented a complete reverse from scores for *The Last Jedi*, which had a critical score of 91 percent fresh but an audience score of 43 percent. In short, critics loved *The Last Jedi* and hated *The Rise of Skywalker*, while fans felt the exact opposite. This state of affairs felt about right for the *Star Wars* universe.

As of February 2020, season 7 of *The Clone Wars* was poised to drop on February 21, and season 2 of *The Mandalorian* was set to be released in October 2020. *Star Wars* appears to be healthy largely due to its television series rather than the movies. Through it all, George Lucas comes and goes like a force ghost, appearing to his young padawans when the force feels out of balance.

# CONCLUSION

## The Cycle Is Complete

When Obi-Wan tells Anakin in *Revenge of the Sith* that he has become the very thing he had sworn to destroy, it is difficult not to consider George Lucas's journey from a young filmmaker interested in destroying the studio system to a studio system unto himself.

From the time Lucas was a young boy, he fought against his father as well as neighborhood bullies. He tried to overcompensate for his inadequacies by behaving recklessly, which nearly got him killed when he totaled his car before graduating from high school. At USC, he challenged the administration and broke the rules to make better films and distinguish himself from his fellow students. In his most notable fight, Lucas took on a weakened old Hollywood system out of touch with the hippie generation and at the mercy of a new generation of American filmmakers with their fingers on the cultural pulse of America. Lucas swore to democratize the filmmaking process, to wrangle the means of production from the studio executives who did not care a lick about quality filmmaking or directors and their unique visions.

After ruthlessly winning his battle with the studios, Lucas created a juggernaut production company in Lucasfilm that re-created the studio system in his own likeness and cemented it when he sold the franchise to Disney, a corporation that put a stranglehold on the most popular cultural franchises in the world. Disney proved to be more like old Hollywood than the American New Wave of the 1970s.

In two of the last five *Star Wars* films, Disney and Lucasfilm executives replaced the directors; in their hands the *Star Wars* film *Solo* lost over $50 million. Disney's plan to indulge *Star Wars* fans with more films and shows than they could handle was almost fatal for the enduring and fetishized franchise. In the *Star Wars* saga, Darth Vader brings balance to the force by killing the Empire in *Return of the Jedi*. A Hollywood ending is unlikely for the story of *Star Wars*, unless one believes Baby Yoda to be the chosen one.

From the moment Qui-Gon Jinn encountered Anakin Skywalker, he realized the boy was special. Only later did Qui-Gon refer to a chosen one, an individual who might bring balance to the force. It was not long before Qui-Gon believed Anakin to be the chosen one, and this belief was strengthened when he and Obi-Wan analyzed Anakin's midichlorian level and discovered that it surpassed even Yoda's. According to Anakin's mother, the boy had no father, suggesting the midichlorians themselves impregnated Anakin's mother in some sort of force-propelled parthenogenetic insemination, a theory later given credence by the Emperor. The idea of parthenogenesis, or virgin birth, reflected the long and fraught history of George Lucas as an asexual man, as well as the manner in which he had his first biological child.

When Qui-Gon insisted that Anakin be trained as a Jedi, the Jedi Council refused, citing fear and darkness in young Anakin. Nevertheless, the Jedi took Anakin in and Obi-Wan trained him. The Jedi were sworn protectors of the Senate and selfless warriors who gave their lives for other people. They defended the democratic Senate that represented all the galaxies and all the beings in the *Star Wars* universe. They were protectors of the weak and marginalized and were free of personal desire, the opposite of the Sith who only craved power. As a Jedi, Anakin swore to fight tyranny directed at the powerless.

Anakin's weaknesses early on were partly related to his guilt about abandoning his mother on Tatooine in order to train to become a Jedi knight. The Jedi Council sensed his guilt and inability to let his mother go. Anakin eventually gave in to his feelings and returned to Tatooine to save his mother, wiping out an entire village of Tusken Raiders, including women and children. Anakin's act was understandable, if not the Jedi way. His mother had been enslaved and died in his arms, and as a result Anakin sought revenge, a characteristic of the Sith, not the Jedi. This sequence of events was a foreboding of another brush with the dark side connected with Padme's forecasted death. Anakin's love of Padme and vision of her death propelled him to investigate the possibility of preventing death, something Chancellor Palpatine promised to teach him.

Anakin was impatient, impetuous, and moody. He was emotional and paranoid. He resented the Jedi Council's unwillingness to confer on him the title of Jedi Master and designate him an official member of the Council. He was jealous of Obi-Wan and bristled whenever Obi-Wan spent time with Padme, all of which the Chancellor took advantage, stoking Anakin's every whim and showering him with sycophantic praise. Eventually when Anakin realized that Palpatine was a Sith Lord, it was too late. He had already grown attached to the Chancellor and prevented the Jedi from killing him by aiding in the destruction of Mace Windu. Anakin could not have it both ways. He could not give in to the Bogan and still maintain healthy relationships with those he loved. Consequently, when his thirst for power reached a feverish pitch, he massacred innocent younglings and choked to death his pregnant wife, the very person for whom he chose the Bogan over the Ashla, fully submitting to the dark side of the force and to the Emperor. In a nearly fatal act, Anakin violently attacked Obi-Wan, his former master, and the closest thing to a brother that he ever had. Once Padme died and Order 66 nearly wiped out all the remaining Jedi, Anakin destroyed everything that he loved and became the very thing he had sworn to destroy. As Vader, he was dehumanized, more machine than man, and utterly reliant on technology for life. He was only later redeemed when he destroyed the Emperor and ultimately brought balance to the force, fulfilling his destiny. Anakin's masculine insecurities in relation to his mother and his wife Padme were driving factors in his turn to the dark side.

The parallels between Darth Vader and George Lucas are striking. Like Anakin, there is an essential goodness in Lucas. What drove him as a young filmmaker was a compassion for filmmaking and a soft spot for the underdog. Despite growing up in an upper-middle-class family and enjoying all the privileges bestowed on a white male from a rich family, Lucas never lost his streak of leftist rebelliousness or his interest in popular struggles.

Like Vader, masculine insecurities drove Lucas for much of his life, causing him to rule over his universe as Vader ruled over his. Early in his life, Lucas turned to car racing as a way to combat his nerdy persona. When he nearly killed himself and totaled his car, his interest soon turned to making films. Film allowed him to reconstruct reality and present himself as a master genius incapable of failure. Despite having a sexless marriage, Lucas gave off the impression that he was a successful lady's man. Evidence of his sexual dysfunction made its way into his movies.

When the old Hollywood studios collapsed in the 1960s, selling their wares to corporations completely ignorant of the movie business, marketing departments looked to young filmmakers to target the burgeoning market share of young people. Amid a tumultuous decade of violence, war, and political scandal, these young filmmakers responded with films that mirrored the gritty, morally gray cultural moment. Lucas emerged amid the confusion as a young filmmaker with a unique vision among visionary filmmakers, a maverick among mavericks. American New Wave directors were tough and masculine lady's men. Even though Lucas and Spielberg were the dorks of the era, they nevertheless attempted to parlay their filmmaking success into masculine supremacy. For the American New Wave, perceived masculinity was important for one's career.

While his first feature film, *THX 1138*, shared many of the same qualities as other 1970s films in its pessimistic view of contemporary culture, his next film took a different tack and attempted to counter pessimism with a nostalgic viewpoint. Lucas once commented that *American Graffiti* was born out of a friendly bet between Francis Ford Coppola and himself as to whether he could make a warm and fuzzy comedy instead of a hard-edged, avant-garde film like *THX 1138*. Lucas accepted the bet and won. When the studios attempted to toy with his films, cutting four minutes from both *THX 1138* and *American Graffiti*, Lucas became enraged. For him, his films were more real than his own life. He had no control over his life, unlike his films. His third film combined elements of his first two films and changed Hollywood forever.

Lucas was not concerned with telling a realistic story about humans in space. He was more interested in making an action film that simply took place in space. Much of science fiction at the time was dystopic and morose. Lucas felt the world was ready for a film about heroes, a film that left audiences feeling positive about the world when they left the theater. He was far from confident. Fearing *Star Wars* would be a flop and concerned that it would be very difficult to make the remaining part of the story that he had already written or at least conceived, Lucas retained the rights to possible sequels as well as merchandising. His plan was to sell merchandise that would promote the film when studios would not. Little did he know that there were scores of young people in the film industry working in model photography and itching to work on a feature science fiction film. Lucas hired many of these young fans of science fiction to work on his film. These brilliant fans of a little-known art form were usually left alone to come up with models based largely on Ralph McQuarrie's art, which helped Lucas get the Fox deal for *Star Wars*. The Death Star, for example, was a 40 × 60 feet model built from scratch. Even the computers at ILM were built from scratch out of word processors. Along with Lucas's hidden workforce was a potential fan base for a science fiction franchise the likes of which the world had never seen.

Carrie Fisher, a strikingly beautiful and sexy woman, said during her audition for the role of Princess Leia that she mostly talked to Brian De Palma, who was casting for his film *Carrie*, because George did not talk. In London the British crew, who under union rules promptly clocked out at 5:30 p.m. sharp every day unless they were in the middle of a shot, bullied Lucas. The rules stipulated that Lucas could ask the crew for an extra five minutes provided they agreed, but they always voted him down. When Lucas tried to make a suggestion about lighting or a camera angle to the lead cameraman, he was told that making those kinds of suggestions was not his job. Fisher also noted that on the set of the first *Star Wars* film, George lost his voice, but because he never said anything anyway, the actors had no idea.[1]

Walter Cronkite credited *Star Wars* with lifting the culture from the depression of the 1970s and steering them toward space.[2] Despite Lucas's desire to break free from the studio system, he more than doubled 20th Century Fox's highest annual profit in the year after the film released. The most profit Fox had made in one year prior to *Star Wars* was $37 million. In 1977–1978, thanks to *Star Wars*, Fox made $79 million in profit.

Although Kenner made a modest deal with Lucasfilm to release a line of action figures prior to the film's release, it did not think the film would be a hit. The toymaker was totally taken off guard and resorted to sending fans a box instead of the toys themselves for Christmas in 1977. The idea that Kenner sent the packaging alone was amazing and forecasted the common practice of toy manufacturers spending more on packaging than the toys themselves in the years to come.

Fans of *Star Wars* came from all walks of life, from the highly educated to the salt of the earth. Lucas democratized an experience of viewing, if not a way of making, films. Fans have compared him to Shakespeare and Homer and extolled his profound genius and terrific impact on global culture. The moment fans began playing with the ubiquitous toys or even the empty box that promised the toys, *Star Wars* participatory culture emerged. Almost immediately, fans wanted to take part in the franchise. Much of the early fan films were parodies, mockeries of the film, a form of bullying that was also a form of flattery. For Lucas, this was a ticking time bomb. Very soon, if not from the very start, aspects of participatory *Star Wars* fan culture were sexual, such as one animated film where C3PO drops his pink panties and propositions Luke, or a live-action film where Ewoks rape women in the forest of Endor.[3] These films enraged Lucas and caused him to come down hard on participatory *Star Wars* fan art. Slash fiction, fan fiction that portrayed same-sex relationships among his popular male characters, particularly troubled Lucas. Once Lucas's first wife Marcia left him, his insecurities only increased.

Lucas began altering his first *Star Wars* films in order to maintain the myth of his genius: that he had conceived *Star Wars* whole, that he birthed it unlike his inability to birth his own children. In effect, he cut off the fingers of his own film children as a menacing parent, not unlike Francisco Goya's painting

*Saturn Devouring His Son*, based on the Greek myth of Titan Cronus who was so fearful that his children would overthrow him, he swallowed each one at birth. When fans first found out that Lucas was remastering the original films, they were excited. Lucas announced that he was interested primarily in preserving the films that had begun to deteriorate, but when fans saw the movies and realized they were different in profound ways, they were furious. For fans, this was a power move that made it clear whose world *Star Wars* actually was. This was the first major blow to *Star Wars* fandom.

No one announced the sorts of changes that were made, such as the Mos Eisley cantina scene with Han and Greedo. Fans were unprepared. They were not interested in seeing a different film. They wanted to see the same film and recapture the feeling they had when they first saw it twenty years before. They wanted to see a better film, not a different film. Many felt as though the movies were no longer Lucas's to change. They had taken on a life of their own within the culture, irrespective of Lucas. The so-called flaws in the films were actually what affected people the most, not unlike the cigarette lodged in one of Jackson Pollock's oil paintings. Fans felt obliged to defend the original films that Lucas seemed to hold in such disdain. They accused Lucas of disrespecting the other filmmakers who worked on the originals and had to make do with what was available and what they could invent under time and financial constraints. When Lucas supplanted some of those innovations with CGI, he undermined Academy Award–winning work. Once fans realized that Lucas's intent was to wipe the originals off the face of the earth, Lucas criminalized his own fandom by outlawing his work. *Star Wars* fans began creating their own digital files from the original laser discs and offering them as free downloads on the internet. They had lost faith in Lucas.

We might look at *Star Wars* fandom as representative of Luke Skywalker, a true nerd son responsible for Vader's destruction and redemption. Both Anakin and Luke were gearhead dorks who longed to leave their remote sand planet. Lucas resembled his own fandom until *Star Wars* became a major hit film and Lucas's own insecurities compelled him to come down hard on fans and alter his films to bolster his own legend. After enduring attacks on their fan art and gritting their teeth as Lucas changed their beloved films around and then forbade them to see the originals, the fans finally had their say with the prequels, mercilessly deriding Lucas and essentially killing the Dark Lord responsible for the *Star Wars* universe. The price Lucas paid for antagonizing his fans and embodying a corporation was seeing fans turn on him. The venom with which fans attacked the prequels was totally irrational and odd. Fans began editing the prequels themselves. This was a natural extension of what had gone on before, starting with the toys. No film franchise had ever courted fan participation like *Star Wars*. No longer was fan fiction or fan films enough—fans wanted access to the canon. Fans wanted to be canonized. For the consummate *Star Wars* nerd, one way to top his fellow nerds was to hate the cherished artifact, to hate *Star Wars*. Hatred of the sacrosanct artifact was now a sign of a deeper kind of love.

In the 2010 documentary film *The People vs. George Lucas*, fans outright compared Lucas to both Darth Vader and Luke Skywalker. One fan noted that there was a day when George Lucas was a scruffy nerf herder from Tatooine. He was one of us, a fan said.[4] Lucas, whose name sounds a lot like Luke, was a science fiction and technology geek like many of his fans. That eventually changed. Lucas once compared himself to Darth Vader, noting, "What I was trying to do was stay independent, so I could make the movies I wanted to make, but at the same time I was fighting the corporate system. . . . But now I've found myself being the head of a corporation, so there's a certain irony there, that I've become the very thing that I was trying to avoid. Which basically is what part of *Star Wars* is about—that is, Darth Vader."[5]

*Star Wars* fans somehow both love and hate *Star Wars* films as well as Lucas. This is a complicated notion, but one that is apparent among the fans. The feeling among many fans is that Lucas abandoned them by committing an unforgivable crime somewhere along the way. He is responsible equally for their joy and their pain. For *Star Wars* fans, it is clear that the films are not just films. Rather, they are inspirational artifacts that promote creativity. And to some, they are a religion.

Perhaps the Emperor all along has been the Disney franchise. If Lucas's main goal when breaking into the film industry was to throttle the studios because he felt they treated filmmakers unfairly, then selling the franchise to Disney was similar to Vader handing his power over to the Emperor, without the likelihood that Lucas would ever throttle the Emperor and restore balance to the force, as Vader eventually does. In this scenario, Lucas was actually worse than the supreme villain that he created. The equivalent of Anakin becoming the mechanized Darth Vader and serving the Emperor was Lucasfilm Disney becoming a *Star Wars* industrial marketing machine.

Lucas once told his father that he would never be a businessman, a man solely concerned with making money. Despite this, he became a producer and entrepreneur. In attempting to destroy the establishment, he became the establishment almost overnight and was destroyed as a filmmaker. Many, including his good friend Francis Ford Coppola, felt the popularity of *Star Wars* deprived the public of more personal avant-garde films that Lucas always said he was going to make. Instead, Lucas provided a global industrial marketing complex.

With the popularity of streaming shows like *The Mandalorian* and *LEGO Star Wars*, the legacy of *Star Wars* may be more visible now outside of the films. For young fans like my ten-year-old son, the movies already rank a distant second to *Star Wars* LEGOs. My son saves up his allowance for *Star Wars* LEGOs. For Christmas, he asked for a nearly $200 LEGO version of the Millennium Falcon. The first *Star Wars* LEGO set appeared in 1999 and, since then, over 230 different LEGO *Star Wars* sets have appeared. *Star Wars* excitement in 2020 centers on the forthcoming seventh season of *The Clone Wars* and season 2 of *The Mandalorian*.

George Lucas has been grappling with machine technology since he was a teenager, maybe even before that. A machine nearly killed him as a young man. Advanced technology compelled him to alter films that fans considered sacred. Technology was largely to blame for much of the criticism he received for the prequels. At the heart of the *Star Wars* story lies a dichotomy between humanity and machine technology represented by the Clones and the droids. In the *Star Wars* universe, both humans and droids are capable of betrayal as well as self-sacrifice. The story of *Star Wars* is the story of nerd culture and its triumph. Like in many great stories, there is tragedy and betrayal, followed by redemption. The redemption has yet to come in the story of *Star Wars*. It is time for George Lucas to come home to nerd culture. Redemption awaits . . .

# NOTES

## PROLOGUE. THE TRIUMPH OF NERD CULTURE

1. "Disneyland's Disastrous Opening Day," History.com, July 17, 2015. https://www.history.com/news/disneylands-disastrous-opening-day-60-years-ago.

2. "Disneyland Opens Gates to Thousands: 15,000 on Hand in Mile-Long Lines as Turnstiles Start," *Los Angeles Times*, July 19, 1955, 2.

3. "Nixon Takes Time Out for Disneyland," *Los Angeles Times*, August 12, 1955, 2.

4. Brian Jay Jones, *George Lucas: A Life* (New York: Little, Brown and Company, 2016), 26.

5. Jones, *George Lucas*, 356.

6. Jones, *George Lucas*, 453–54.

7. Chris Taylor, *How Star Wars Conquered the Universe: The Past, Present, and Future of a Multibillion Dollar Franchise* (New York: Basic Books, 2014), 381.

8. Quoted in Taylor, *How Star Wars Conquered*, 390.

9. Taylor, *How Star Wars Conquered*, 392.

10. Ben Fritz and Richard Verrier, "Disney Adds *Star Wars* to Its Galaxy: The Big-Bucks Deal for Lucasfilm Will Enable It to Exploit the Film Series Through Sequels, TV, and Theme Parks," *Los Angeles Times*, October 31, 2012, A1.

11. Neal Gabler, "The Triumph of the Brand: Disney's Interest Is in a Built-in Market, Not Fine Filmmaking," *Los Angeles Times*, November 11, 2012, D5.

12. Taylor, *How Star Wars Conquered*, 269.

## CHAPTER 1. AREN'T YOU A LITTLE SHORT FOR A STORMTROOPER?

1. Brian Jay Jones, *George Lucas: A Life* (New York: Little, Brown and Company, 2016), 41.
2. Jones, *George Lucas*, 19.
3. Jones, *George Lucas*, 17.
4. John Baxter, *George Lucas: A Biography* (London: HarperCollins, 1999), 24.
5. Dale Pollock, *Skywalking: The Life and Films of George Lucas*, updated ed. (New York: Da Capo Press, 1999), 16.
6. Sally Kline, ed., *George Lucas Interviews* (Jackson: University Press of Mississippi, 1999), 43.
7. Pollock, *Skywalking*, 29.
8. Jones, *George Lucas*, 22.
9. Jones, *George Lucas*, 18.
10. Jones, *George Lucas*, 29.
11. Jones, *George Lucas*, 18–19.
12. Pollock, *Skywalking*, 28.
13. Baxter, *George Lucas*, 27.
14. Chris Taylor, *How Star Wars Conquered the Universe: The Past, Present, and Future of a Multibillion Dollar Franchise* (New York: Basic Books, 2014), 13.
15. Jones, *George Lucas*, 40.
16. Jones, *George Lucas*, 41.
17. Jones, *George Lucas*, 46.
18. Baxter, *George Lucas*, 49–50.
19. Baxter, *George Lucas*, 57.
20. Taylor, *How Star Wars Conquered*, 49.
21. Jones, *George Lucas*, 62.
22. Jones, *George Lucas*, 64–65.
23. Michael Kaminski, *The Secret History of Star Wars: The Art of Storytelling and the Making of a Modern Epic* (Kingston: Legacy Books Press, 2008), 22–23.
24. Pollock, *Skywalking*, 46.
25. Kline, *George Lucas Interviews*, 20.
26. Baxter, *George Lucas*, 64–65.
27. Jones, *George Lucas*, 77.
28. Jones, *George Lucas*, 66.
29. Jones, *George Lucas*, 81.
30. Baxter, *George Lucas*, 75.
31. Pollock, *Skywalking*, 68.
32. Jones, *George Lucas*, 92.
33. Jones, *George Lucas*, 81–83.
34. Jones, *George Lucas*, 82.
35. Jones, *George Lucas*, 85.

## CHAPTER 2. THESE AREN'T THE DROIDS YOU'RE LOOKING FOR

1. Peter Biskind, *Easy Riders, Raging Bulls: How the Sex-Drugs-and-Rock 'n' Roll Generation Saved Hollywood* (New York: Simon & Shuster, 1998), 15.
2. Biskind, *Easy Riders*, 16.
3. Biskind, *Easy Riders*, 16.
4. Biskind, *Easy Riders*, 243.
5. Biskind, *Easy Riders*, 243.
6. Biskind, *Easy Riders*, 74.
7. "Playboy Interview: Jack Nicholson," *Playboy*, April 1, 1972, 75.
8. Biskind, *Easy Riders*, 338–39.
9. Biskind, *Easy Riders*, 260.
10. Biskind, *Easy Riders*, 256.
11. Brian Jay Jones, *George Lucas: A Life* (New York: Little, Brown and Company, 2016), 89–91.
12. Jones, *George Lucas*, 386.
13. Biskind, *Easy Riders*, 75.
14. Biskind, *Easy Riders*, 258.
15. John Baxter, *George Lucas: A Biography* (London: HarperCollins, 1999), 333–34.
16. Jones, *George Lucas*, 81.
17. Jones, *George Lucas*, 114.
18. Baxter, *George Lucas*, 100.
19. Baxter, *George Lucas*, 100.
20. Dale Pollock, *Skywalking: The Life and Films of George Lucas*, updated ed. (New York: Da Capo Press, 1999), 96.
21. Baxter, *George Lucas*, 118.
22. Jones, *George Lucas*, 156–57.
23. Baxter, *George Lucas*, 32.
24. Baxter, *George Lucas*, 33.
25. Quoted in Jones, *George Lucas*, 161.
26. Jones, *George Lucas*, 161.
27. Alain Silver and James Ursini, *Film Noir Reader* (New York: Limelight, 1996), 112–13.
28. Foster Hirsch, *The Dark Side of the Screen* (Cambridge, MA: Da Capo Press, 1981), 9.
29. Jones, *George Lucas*, 175.
30. Jones, *George Lucas*, 212.
31. Jones, *George Lucas*, 168.
32. Jones, *George Lucas*, 233.
33. Jones, *George Lucas*, 201.
34. Jones, *George Lucas*, 202.

35. Jones, *George Lucas*, 202–3.

36. Jones, *George Lucas*, 204.

37. Jones, *George Lucas*, 223.

38. Biskind, *Easy Riders*, 316.

39. Biskind, *Easy Riders*, 321.

40. Biskind, *Easy Riders*, 324.

41. Jones, *George Lucas*, 239.

42. Jones, *George Lucas*, 247.

43. Jones, *George Lucas*, 261–62.

44. Jones, *George Lucas*, 206.

45. Jones, *George Lucas*, 160.

46. Jones, *George Lucas*, 241.

47. Jones, *George Lucas*, 177.

48. Jones, *George Lucas*, 242.

49. Jones, *George Lucas*, 249.

50. Jones, *George Lucas*, 308.

51. Chris Taylor, *How Star Wars Conquered the Universe: The Past, Present, and Future of a Multibillion Dollar Franchise* (New York: Basic Books, 2014), 259.

52. Quoted in Jones, *George Lucas*, 249.

53. Taylor, *How Star Wars Conquered*, 98–99.

54. Jones, *George Lucas*, 394.

55. Matei Calinescu, *Five Faces of Modernity: Modernism Avant-Garde Decadence Kitsch Postmodernism* (Durham, NC: Duke University Press, 1987), 104.

56. Calinescu, *Five Faces of Modernity*, 111.

57. Calinescu, *Five Faces of Modernity*, 119.

58. *Easy Riders, Raging Bulls: How the Sex, Drugs & Rock 'N' Roll Generation Saved Hollywood*, directed by Kenneth Bowser, DVD (BBC, 2003).

## CHAPTER 3. I HAVE A BAD FEELING ABOUT THIS

1. Benjamin Nugent, *American Nerd: The Story of My People* (New York: Scribner, 2008), 39.

2. Nugent, *American Nerd*, 40–43.

3. Mark Duffet, *Understanding Fandom: An Introduction to the Study of Media Fan Culture* (New York: Bloomsbury, 2013), 9.

4. Duffet, *Understanding Fandom*, 6.

5. Duffet, *Understanding Fandom*, 7.

6. Duffet, *Understanding Fandom*, 5.

7. Henry Jenkins, *Textual Poachers: Television Fans and Participatory Culture*, 2nd Edition (New York: Routledge, 2012), 12.

8. Nugent, *American Nerd*, 55.

9. David Anderegg. *Nerds: How Dorks, Dweebs, Techies, and Trekkies Can Save The World* (New York: Penguin, 2011), 5–6.

10. Anderegg, *Nerds*, 62–66.

11. Anderegg, *Nerds*, 90.

12. John Baxter, *George Lucas: A Biography* (London: HarperCollins, 1999), 333–34.

13. Chris Taylor, *How Star Wars Conquered the Universe: The Past, Present, and Future of a Multibillion Dollar Franchise* (New York: Basic Books, 2014), 173.

14. Taylor, *How Star Wars Conquered*, 184.

15. Dale Pollock, *Skywalking: The Life and Films of George Lucas*, updated ed. (New York: Da Capo, 1999), 195.

16. Michael Kaminski, *The Secret History of Star Wars: The Art of Storytelling and the Making of a Modern Epic* (Kingston: Legacy, 2008), 148.

17. Cass R. Sunstein, *The World According to Star Wars* (New York: HarperCollins, 2016), 58.

18. Kaminski, *The Secret History*, 147.

19. Kaminski, *The Secret History*, 150.

20. Pollock, *Skywalking*, 192–93.

21. Baxter, *George Lucas*, 170–71.

22. Will Brooker, *Using the Force: Creativity, Community, and Star Wars Fans* (New York: Continuum, 2002), 12.

23. Taylor, *How Star Wars Conquered*, 201.

24. Taylor, *How Star Wars Conquered*, 200–2.

25. Brian Jay Jones, *George Lucas: A Life* (New York: Little, Brown and Company, 2016), 259.

26. Taylor, *How Star Wars Conquered*, 241.

27. Pollock, *Skywalking*, 199.

28. Kaminski, *The Secret History*, 190.

29. A shortened form of "retroactive continuity," a term popular in comic book writing.

30. Pollock, *Skywalking*, 211.

31. Pollock, *Skywalking*, 218.

32. Jones, *George Lucas*, 289.

33. Quoted in Baxter, *George Lucas*, 304.

34. Baxter, *George Lucas*, 304.

35. Jones, *George Lucas*, 265.

36. Baxter, *George Lucas*, 327.

37. Jones, *George Lucas*, 303.

38. Jones, *George Lucas*, 304.

39. Jones, *George Lucas*, 310.

40. Jones, *George Lucas*, 312.

41. Jones, *George Lucas*, 312.

42. Quoted in Taylor, *How Star Wars Conquered*, 278.

## CHAPTER 4. A GREAT DISTURBANCE IN THE FORCE

1. Brian Jay Jones, *George Lucas: A Life* (New York: Little, Brown and Company, 2016), 348.

2. John Baxter, *George Lucas: A Biography* (London: HarperCollins, 1999), 10.

3. Baxter, *George Lucas*, 12.

4. Jones, *George Lucas*, 300.

5. Jones, *George Lucas*, 350.

6. Jones, *George Lucas*, 351.

7. Brian Masters. *The Shrine of Jeffrey Dahmer* (London: Hodder and Stoughton, 1993), 125.

8. Quoted in Jones, *George Lucas*, 384.

9. Quoted in Jones, *George Lucas*, 385.

10. Dale Pollock, *Skywalking: The Life and Films of George Lucas*, updated ed. (New York: Da Capo Press, 1999), 2.

11. Jones, *George Lucas*, 22.

12. Will Brooker, *Using the Force: Creativity, Community and Star Wars Fans* (New York: Continuum, 2002), 129.

13. Brooker, *Using the Force*, 165.

14. Brooker, *Using the Force*, 130.

15. Brooker, *Using the Force*, 142–43.

16. Brooker, *Using the Force*, 166.

17. Henry Jenkins, *Textual Poachers: Television Fans and Participatory Culture*, 2nd ed. (New York: Routledge, 2012), 81.

18. Gayle Feyrer, *The Cosmic Collected* (self-published, 1986).

19. "Plato's Stepchildren," *Star Trek: The Original Series*, season 3, episode 10, November 22, 1968.

## CHAPTER 5. I AM ALTERING THE DEAL

1. Chris Taylor, *How Star Wars Conquered the Universe: The Past, Present, and Future of a Multibillion Dollar Franchise* (New York: Basic Books, 2014), 297.

2. Taylor, *How Star Wars Conquered*, 298.

3. Brian Jay Jones, *George Lucas: A Life* (New York: Little, Brown and Company, 2016), 383.

4. Taylor, *How Star Wars Conquered*, 300.

5. Jones, *George Lucas*, 396.

6. Taylor, *How Star Wars Conquered*, 309.

7. Taylor, *How Star Wars Conquered*, 309.

8. Quoted in Taylor, *How Star Wars Conquered*, 312.

9. Jones, *George Lucas*, 390.

10. Taylor, *How Star Wars Conquered*, 316.

11. Taylor, *How Star Wars Conquered*, 326.

12. Taylor, *How Star Wars Conquered*, 327.

13. Peter W. Lee, *A Galaxy Here and Now: Historical and Cultural Readings of Star Wars* (Jefferson, NC: McFarland 2016), 214.

14. Will Brooker, *Using the Force: Creativity, Community and Star Wars Fans* (New York: Continuum, 2002), 167.

15. Henry Jenkins, *Textual Poachers: Television Fans and Participatory Culture*, 2nd ed. (New York: Routledge, 2012), xxvi.

16. Reviews quoted in Taylor, *How Star Wars Conquered*, 331.

17. Taylor, *How Star Wars, Conquered*, 331.

18. Taylor, *How Star Wars Conquered*, 365–66.

19. Michael Kaminski, *The Secret History of Star Wars: The Art of Storytelling and the Making of a Modern Epic* (Kingston: Legacy Books Press, 2008), 373–74.

20. Jones, *George Lucas*, 404.

21. Jones, *George Lucas*, 404–5.

22. Brooker, *Using the Force*, 169.

23. Henry Jenkins, *Convergence Culture*, (New York University Press, 2006), 154–55.

24. Diane Williams, "Star Wars: Come What May," video, July 11, 2012. https://www.youtube.com/watch?v=wpEcJUbssDQ

25. Taylor, *How Star Wars Conquered*, 62.

26. Quoted in Jenkins, *Convergence Culture*,149.

27. Jenkins, *Convergence Culture*, 1551.

28. Jenkins, *Convergence Culture*, 152–53.

29. Quoted in Jones, *George Lucas*, 423.

30. Jones, *George Lucas*, 423.

31. Brooker, *Using the Force*, 90.

32. Jones, *George Lucas*, 432.

33. Jones, *George Lucas*, 436.

34. *Zack and Miri Make a Porno*, directed by Kevin Smith, DVD (Weinstein Co., 2009).

35. Taylor, *How Star Wars Conquered*, 374.

36. Gleiberman and Ebert quoted in Taylor, *How Star Wars Conquered*, 378.

37. Taylor, *How Star Wars Conquered*, 378.

38. Taylor, *How Star Wars Conquered*, 409.

## CHAPTER 6. THIS IS THE WAY

1. Brian Jay Jones, *George Lucas: A Life* (New York: Little, Brown and Company, 2016), 462.

2. Jones, *George Lucas*, 518.

3. Chris Taylor, *How Star Wars Conquered the Universe: The Past, Present, and Future of a Multibillion Dollar Franchise* (New York: Basic Books, 2014), 392.

4. Taylor, *How Star Wars Conquered*, 407.

5. Taylor, *How Star Wars Conquered*, 409.

6. Jones, *George Lucas*, 464.

7. Jones, *George Lucas*, 468.

8. Jones, *George Lucas*, 468.

9. Jones, *George Lucas*, 469.

10. Jones, *George Lucas*, 469.

11. Taylor, *How Star Wars Conquered*, 382.

12. Taylor, *How Star Wars Conquered*, 383.

13. Michael Hiltzik, "Why *Star Wars* Stinks," *Los Angeles Times*, December 30, 2015, C1.

14. Ann Friedman, "Why Did I Pay $30 to See *Star Wars*?" *Los Angeles Times*, December 23, 2015, A13.

15. Mark Newbold, "Mark Hamill Regrets the Death of Han Solo in *The Force Awakens*," Fantha Tracks, June 18, 2019.

16. Josh Rottenburg, "*Rogue One* Rebels Against Type," *Chicago Tribune*, December 16, 2016, 7.

17. Ryan Couch, "Tony Gilroy on *Rogue One* Reshoots: They Were in Terrible Trouble," *Hollywood Reporter*, April 5, 2018.

18. Josh Rottenburg, "'Making *Star Wars* Is a Team Sport': *Rogue One* Director Gareth Edwards on Reshoots, Inspiration, and Trepidation." *Los Angeles Times*, December 8, 2016.

19. Rottenburg, "*Rogue One*," 7.

20. Rottenburg, "*Rogue One*," 7.

21. Anthony Wonke, "The Director and the Jedi," *The Last Jedi*, directed by Rian Johnson, DVD bonus content (Lucasfilm, 2017).

22. Wonke, "The Director and the Jedi."

23. Wonke, "The Director and the Jedi."

24. Scott Mendelson, "Why Do So Many 'Star Wars' Fans Hate 'The Last Jedi'?" *Forbes*, December 19, 2017.

25. Jen Yamato, "A New Hope for Han Solo Film? Ron Howard Is Taking Over *Star Wars* Spinoff Days After Firing of Its Directors," *Los Angeles Times*, June 23, 2017, E1.

26. Yamato, "A New Hope for Han Solo Film?" E1.

27. Ryan Faughnder, "Is *Solo* Dud a Sign of Franchise Fatigue? Subpar Sales Have Some Nervous about Future of *Star Wars*," *Los Angeles Times*, June 5, 2018, C1.

28. Steven Zeitchik, "How Disney Could Get *Star Wars* Back on Track," *Washington Post*, May 29, 2018.

29. Zack Sharf, "'*Solo*' One Year Later: Ron Howard on Internet Trolls, Bad Release Date, and Lord & Miller Feedback," *IndieWire*, May 30, 2019.

30. Erik Kain, "*Star Wars* Is Taking a Break after 'Episode IX'—Even Mark Hamill Has Franchise Fatigue," *Forbes*, April 12, 2019.

31. Mark Duffet, *Understanding Fandom: An Introduction to the Study of Media Fan Culture* (New York: Bloomsbury, 2013), 48.

32. William Mullally, "Here's What George Lucas and Jon Favreau Have Been Talking About for *The Mandalorian*," GQ Middle East, July 25, 2019.

33. Zaki Hasan, "Everyone Loves *The Mandalorian*. For Now," Datebook.com, November 15, 2019.

34. Erik Kain, "*The Mandalorian* Season 1 Review: The Best New *Star Wars* since *Return of the Jedi*," *Forbes*, December 28, 2019.

35. Zack Sharf, "Martin Scorsese Compares Marvel Movies to Theme Parks: 'That's Not Cinema,'" *IndieWire*, October 4, 2019.

36. Brian Lowry, "*Star Wars: The Rise of Skywalker* Rises to the Occasion of Concluding the Epic Saga," CNN.com, December 18, 2019.

37. Brian Grimm, "A Spent Force: The End of the *Star Wars* Saga Stinks Like a Womp Rat's Ass," *Tucson Weekly*, December 26, 2019.

## CONCLUSION. THE CYCLE IS COMPLETE

1. *Empire of Dreams: The Story of the Star Wars Trilogy*, directed by Edith Becker and Kevin Burns (Lucasfilm, 2004).

2. *Empire of Dreams*.

3. *The People vs. George Lucas*, directed by Alexandre O. Philippe (Lionsgate, 2010). DVD.

4. *The People vs. George Lucas*.

5. Sean Guynes and Dan Hassler-Forest, eds., *Star Wars and the History of Transmedia Storytelling* (Amsterdam: Amsterdam University Press, 2018), 40.

# REFERENCES

Anderegg, David. *Nerds: How Dorks, Dweebs, Techies, and Trekkies Can Save the World*. New York: Penguin, 2011.

Baxter, John. *George Lucas: A Biography*. London: HarperCollins, 1999.

Biskind, Peter. *Easy Riders, Raging Bulls: How the Sex-Drugs-and-Rock 'n' Roll Generation Saved Hollywood*. New York: Simon & Shuster, 1998.

Brooker, Will. *Using the Force: Creativity, Community, and Star Wars Fans*. New York: Continuum, 2002.

Calinescu, Matei. *Five Faces of Modernity: Modernism Avant-Garde Decadence Kitsch Postmodernism*. Durham, NC: Duke University Press, 1987.

Couch, Ryan. "Tony Gilroy on *Rogue One* Reshoots: They Were in 'Terrible Trouble.'" *Hollywood Reporter*, April 5, 2018. https://www.hollywoodreporter.com/heat-vision/star-wars-rogue-one-writer-tony-gilroy-opens-up-reshoots-1100060.

"Disneyland Opens Gates to Thousands: 15,000 on Hand in Mile-Long Lines as Turnstiles Start." *Los Angeles Times*, July 19, 1955.

"Disneyland's Disastrous Opening Day." History.com, July 17, 2015. https://www.history.com/news/disneylands-disastrous-opening-day-60-years-ago

Duffet, Mark. *Understanding Fandom: An Introduction to the Study of Media Fan Culture*. New York: Bloomsbury, 2013.

*Easy Riders, Raging Bulls: How The Sex, Drugs & Rock 'N' Roll Generation Saved Hollywood*. Directed by Kenneth Bowser. DVD. BBC, 2003.

*Empire of Dreams: The Story of the Star Wars Trilogy*. Directed by Edith Becker and Kevin Burns. Lucasfilm, 2004.

Faughnder, Ryan. "Is *Solo* Dud a Sign of Franchise Fatigue? Subpar Sales Have Some Nervous about Future of *Star Wars*." *Los Angeles Times*, June 5, 2018.

Feyrer, Gayle. *The Cosmic Collected*. Self-published, 1986.

Friedman, Ann. "Why Did I Pay $30 to See *Star Wars*? *Los Angeles Times*, December 23, 2015.

Fritz, Ben, and Richard Verrier. "Disney Adds *Star Wars* to Its Galaxy; The Big-Bucks Deal for Lucasfilm Will Enable It to Exploit the Film Series through Sequels, TV, and Theme Parks." *Los Angeles Times*, October 31, 2012.

Gabler, Neal. "The Triumph of the Brand: Disney's Interest Is in a Built-in Market, Not Fine Filmmaking." *Los Angeles Times*, November 11, 2012.

Grimm, Brian. "A Spent Force: The End of the *Star Wars* Saga Stinks like a Womp Rat's Ass." *Tucson Weekly*, December 26, 2019.

Guynes, Sean, and Dan Hassler-Forest, eds. *Star Wars and the History of Transmedia Storytelling*. Amsterdam: Amsterdam University Press, 2018.

Hasan, Zaki. "Everyone Loves *The Mandalorian* for Now." *Datebook*, November 15, 2019. https://datebook.sfchronicle.com/movies-tv/california-streamin-everyone -loves-the-mandalorian-for-now.

Hiltzik, Michael. "Why *Star Wars* Stinks." *Los Angeles Times*, December 30, 2015.

Hirsch, Foster. *The Dark Side of the Screen*. Cambridge, MA: Da Capo Press, 1981.

Jenkins, Henry. *Convergence Culture*. New York: New York University Press, 2006.

———. *Textual Poachers: Television Fans and Participatory Culture*. 2nd ed. New York: Routledge, 2012.

Jones, Brian Jay. *George Lucas: A Life*. New York: Little, Brown and Company, 2016.

Kain, Erik. "*The Mandalorian* Season 1 Review: The Best New *Star Wars* since *Return of the Jedi*." *Forbes*, December 28, 2019. https://www.forbes.com/sites/erik kain/2019/12/28/the-mandalorian-season-1-review-the-best-new-star-wars-since -return-of-the-jedi/#4122a694572b.

———. "*Star Wars* Is Taking a Break after 'Episode IX'—Even Mark Hamill Has Franchise Fatigue." *Forbes*, April 12, 2019. https://www.forbes.com/sites/erik kain/2019/04/12/star-wars-is-going-on-hiatus-after-episode-ix—even-mark-hamill -has-franchise-fatigue/#108f2e24d509.

Kaminski, Michael. *The Secret History of Star Wars: The Art of Storytelling and the Making of a Modern Epic*. Kingston: Legacy Books Press, 2008.

Kline, Sally, ed. *George Lucas Interviews*. Jackson: University Press of Mississippi, 1999.

Lee, Peter W. *A Galaxy Here and Now: Historical and Cultural Readings of Star Wars*. Jefferson, NC: McFarland, 2016.

Lowry, Brian. "*Star Wars: The Rise of Skywalker* Rises to the Occasion of Concluding the Epic Saga." CNN.com, December 18, 2019. https://www.cnn.com/2019/12/18/ entertainment/star-wars-the-rise-of-skywalker-review/index.html.

Masters, Brian. *The Shrine of Jeffrey Dahmer*. London: Hodder and Stoughton, 1993.

Mendelson, Scott. "Why Do So Many 'Star Wars' Fans Hate 'The Last Jedi'?" *Forbes*, December 19, 2017. https://www.forbes.com/sites/scottmendelson/2017/12/19/the -last-jedi-why-star-wars-fans-hate-one-of-the-best-star-wars-movies/#6e859d685658.

Mullally, William. "Here's What George Lucas and Jon Favreau Have Been Talking About For *The Mandalorian*." *GQ Middle East*, July 25, 2019. https://www.gqmid

dleeast.com/culture/heres-what-jon-favreau-and-george-lucas-have-been-talking
-about-for-the-mandalorian.

Newbold, Mark. "Mark Hamill Regrets the Death of Han Solo in *The Force Awakens*."
*Fantha Tracks*, June 18, 2019. https://www.fanthatracks.com/news/film-music-tv/
mark-hamill-regrets-the-death-of-han-solo-in-the-force-awakens/.

"Nixon Takes Time Out for Disneyland: Vice-President and Family Prove to Be Top
Attractions." *Los Angeles Times*, August 12, 1955.

Nugent, Benjamin. *American Nerd: The Story of My People*. New York: Scribner, 2008.

*The People vs. George Lucas*. Directed by Alexandre O. Philippe. DVD. Lionsgate,
2010.

"Plato's Stepchildren." *Star Trek: The Original Series*. Season 3, episode 10. November
22, 1968.

"Playboy Interview: Jack Nicholson." *Playboy*, April 1, 1972.

Pollock, Dale. *Skywalking: The Life and Films of George Lucas*. Updated ed. New York:
Da Capo Press, 1999.

Rottenburg, Josh. "'Making *Star Wars* Is a Team Sport': *Rogue One* Director Gareth
Edwards On Reshoots, Inspiration, and Trepidation." *Los Angeles Times*, December
8, 2016.

———. "*Rogue One* Rebels Against Type." *Chicago Tribune*, December 16, 2016.

Sharf, Zack. "Martin Scorsese Compares Marvel Movies to Theme Parks: 'That's Not
Cinema.'" *IndieWire*, October 4, 2019.

———. "'*Solo*' One Year Later: Ron Howard on Internet Trolls, Bad Release Date, and
Lord & Miller Feedback." *IndieWire*, May 30, 2019.

Silver, Alain, and James Ursini. *Film Noir Reader*. New York: Limelight, 1996.

Sunstein, Cass R. *The World According to Star Wars*. New York: HarperCollins, 2016.

Taylor, Chris. *How Star Wars Conquered the Universe: The Past, Present, and Future of
a Multibillion Dollar Franchise*. New York: Basic Books, 2014.

Williams, Diane. "Star Wars: Come What May." video, July 11, 2012. https://www
.youtube.com/watch?v=wpEcJUbssDQ.

Wonke, Anthony. "The Director and the Jedi." *The Last Jedi*. Directed by Rian Johnson. DVD Bonus Content. Lucasfilm, 2017.

Yamato, Jen. "A New Hope for Han Solo film? Ron Howard Is Taking Over *Star Wars*
Spinoff Days After Firing of Its Directors." *Los Angeles Times*, June 23, 2017.

*Zack and Miri Make a Porno*. Directed by Kevin Smith. DVD. Weinstein Co., 2009.

Zeitchik, Steven. "How Disney Could Get *Star Wars* Back on Track." *Washington
Post*, May 29, 2018.

# INDEX

# ABOUT THE AUTHOR

**Josef Benson** is associate professor of literatures and languages at the University of Wisconsin–Parkside. He is the author of *J. D. Salinger's* The Catcher in the Rye: *A Cultural History* (Rowman & Littlefield, 2018) and *Hypermasculinities in the Contemporary Novel: Cormac McCarthy, Toni Morrison, and James Baldwin* (Rowman & Littlefield, 2014).